Don't Disturb my pond

By. Cameron M. Vance

Don't Disturb My Pond

Paperback ISBN: 979-8-9851394-5-7

Online ISBN: 979-8-9851394-6-4

LCCN: 2022920650

First printing edition, 2022. Publisher: PO Box 1082, Logan, OH, 43138 cameronmvance.family.blog

Table of Contents

INTRODUCTION

In 2022, my spouse and I went on a vacation to Peru. I frequently traveled to visit new places each year, but this particular trip was among my favorites. I was inspired by a pond in Peru, a country known for its old wisdom and rich legacy.

The body, mind, and soul make up every individual. We place high importance on the health of our body to be free from illness and diseases, but have we ever given our mind wellbeing any thought?

Like a pond, the mind is subject to internal and external factors that result in bubbles, clutter, and ripples that disturb its tranquility. Calming your mind is the mental state of peace of mind, being free from agitation, negative self-talk, or disturbance. It is being at peace with oneself or in a calm state of consciousness.

Your mind is capable of recalling earlier experiences and occurrences. Your mind is also capable of planning forward and thinking about the future. You might think about unpleasant things and traumatic events from the past, as well as happy memories and exciting things that will happen in the future. The only thing that is permanent in this world is change. Millions of cells regularly die in the body, producing millions more. Your mind's perceptions, thoughts, ideas, and opinions change constantly.

Your state of mind frequently directly impacts your success or failure. A focused mind has limitless potential, whereas a distracted mind severely limits all possibilities. Therefore, the secret to attaining all that one sets out to is to calm an agitated mind.

This book is for those looking for ways to clear their minds of the clutter, limiting beliefs, and the like. This book will guide you to change your mindset and reframe your thoughts to attract calmness and accomplish your dreams!

THE POND: THE MIND

Our life is the expression of our thoughts - **Buddha.**

The pond was tranquil. At the bottom, rocks and pebbles rested quietly. Small fish swam lazily about. On the mirror-like surface, trees were sharply reflected. All was tranquil, but not for long; a hungry fish leaped out of the water, causing disturbance to the once calm pond. The frogs and roseate skimmer leaping, diving, and flapping on the pond, causing ripples in successive circles. The once-still reflection of the trees became so distorted and jagged that their form was no longer recognizable. As the waves approached the bank, they gradually diminished.

Comparable to the pond is the mind. When something - sight, sound, touch, thought, or emotion - comes into contact with an untrained mind, it trembles, shakes, waves, and ruffles. The mind gets dark and foggy; the mind's turbulence muddles our thoughts and judgment; our behavior and reaction mirror what is seething beneath. Mind's ripples can persist for a short time or much longer if we hold on to them unintentionally or due

7

to a lack of awareness and are unable to let go naturally.

Thoughts resemble fish, stones, and invasive species in that they disturb the water and cause ripples and waves. In the absence of clear vision, water must be stirred. And with constant inputs from society, individuals, technology, and social media. It is tough to maintain mental composure. It's as if stones are constantly pelting the mind. Even during sleep, the mind continues to process thoughts.

Mental activity is the source of perceived anxiety and stress. An idea or emotion can generate ripples that spin the mind circles without knowing when to stop. Rather than taking the time to comprehend the source, we frequently choose a quick remedy to alleviate the symptoms. We distract the mind from anxiety, despair, and anger by engaging in more enjoyable activities. The only thing we retain from experience is the agony we endured. Each time we press the rewind button on a thought, we cement that suffering in our long-term memory. Our wounds are asleep, awaiting the next available occasion to awaken. Once the waves have settled, it is too late. We have already lost our mental equilibrium.

What is the power of the human mind? It appears that we do not know the limitations of the human intellect; instead, we expect or guess them. Also, there are those among us, let's call them super-beings, who can accomplish things with their brains that others cannot. It appears that the human mind can achieve practically everything it sets out to do and maybe reprogrammed by its owner if so desired.

As it is commonly stated that "what you think, you become," your mind becomes more adept at whatever you practice thinking about. As many neurologists believe, the mind is comparable to a muscle; "if you don't use it, you lose it."

Occasionally, memories of long-past years, sadness, and pain may return, like fish swimming to the surface of a pond and blowing bubbles. Both external and internal forces can influence the mind. The arising ideas and feelings will soon pass away on their own. There is no need to reject, discard, or conceal them. Observe as they come and depart. Learn from their mistakes.

The frogs, Roseate skimmers and fish have submerged. The pond restores its tranquility. The tree's reflection reappears. If you attempt to take control of these frogs, Roseate skimmers and fish or organize them to your liking, they will battle to escape. Your mental pond will gradually get more chaotic, filthy, and murky. You may stumble into it.

The mind is only occupied with unresolved thoughts and emotions. And the majority of unsolved emotional difficulties are not actual problems at all; they are merely our circling ideas. Observing the mind reveals that each bothersome thought or feeling has a beginning, a middle, and an end. Occasionally, the mind will jump to something else before you even conclude. When ideas and emotions are seen frequently, and for an extended time without judgment, the mind quickly becomes accustomed to them, assuming no more thoughts are added and disappear naturally. One tends to lose interest in it if it is boring and predictable, just like anything else. Likewise, the mind will become less preoccupied with predictable thoughts and emotions. The mind relaxes because it comprehends!

A lesson learned results in a shift in perspective and conduct. This means we will not repeat the error of allowing the past to confine our minds and prevent us from moving forward. Our thoughts and feelings become less troublesome. If not, we have learned nothing! This requires practice and instruction. As each idea or emotion comes, you must be actively aware of what you are thinking and experiencing. Without awareness, you are liable to become disoriented, engulfed, and drowned in them.

Occasionally, not just frogs, Roseate skimmers, and fish generate a ripple. A mild wind or a raindrop can do the same function, but to a smaller extent. Our mission is to mindfully observe, comprehend, and let the pond of our mind return to its tranquility.

The human mind comprises two distinct parts: the subconscious and the conscious.

Conscious mind.

The most fundamental definition of the conscious mind is the portion of the mind you are aware of. It regulates your voluntary thoughts and actions. For instance, I want you to raise your left hand in the air right now. That's a voluntary function, which is regulated by your conscious mind.

Additionally, the conscious mind is the reasoning portion of your mind. It is the part of your mind that can examine a situation logically and make decisions based on the facts. Similarly, your conscious mind operates by examining prior errors and learning from them. Setting objectives for the future is another instance in which your conscious mind is active. Occasionally, you may hear someone say, "I took a deliberate decision to do that." Such is the capacity of the conscious mind. It enables us to assess the situation, evaluate the facts, assess the dangers, and determine what we perceive to be the most prudent course of action. It also enables us to formulate a well-considered implementation strategy for our chosen course of action. However magnificent the conscious mind may be, it has intrinsic limitations.

For one thing, the conscious mind's memory is limited. How frequently have you had problems remembering someone's name or where you placed your keys? These examples illustrate the limited capacity of the conscious mind's memory.

Another limit of the conscious mind is that it cannot perform multiple tasks simultaneously. If it attempts to perform multiple tasks simultaneously, it must rapidly switch between them. An example would be reading while someone else is speaking. At some moment, your conscious mind can either focus on what you are reading or on what is being said.

However, it cannot focus on both at once. Consistent with what the term "conscious" indicates, the conscious mind is incapable of doing anything that it is not "consciously" focused on at any given time.

Subconscious Mind

The subconscious mind is always active 24 hours a day and may perform an infinite number of tasks simultaneously. It's as if a computer is continuously operating in the background of your mind, managing your automatic processes, emotions, and habits. Whether wide awake or deep asleep, your subconscious mind controls all your body's critical operations without your conscious mind's assistance.

To breathe, to make your heart beat, to digest your food, to blink your eyes and more, requires no conscious thought. Your subconscious mind handles all of this for you 24/7, whether awake or asleep. Your subconscious mind continually communicates with every cell in your body, getting information from them and sending them commands. In addition, the subconscious mind handles all the mundane activities you must diligently learn with your conscious mind.

Consider the time when you first learned to drive. Initially, you had to consider every action you took deliberately. In High school, I remembered teaching my friend how to drive. I had to say things like, "At the next intersection, we will turn right. Take your foot off the gas, activate your right blinker, step on the brake, rotate the steering wheel to the right, straighten the steering wheel, take your foot off the brake, and step back on the gas."

In other words, she had to consider and be trained on every action carefully. But once she completed the conscious learning process, neural pathways were built in her brain, and her subconscious mind gradually took over. Hence, she no longer had to consider every action or movement consciously. Today, she is an outstanding driver, and her subconscious mind controls most of her driving.

The same approach applies to most things you have consciously learned, such as riding a bicycle, tying your shoes, swimming, etc. These are all examples of things you had to learn consciously, through a laborious process; yet, once you completed this conscious process, your subconscious mind took over, and you can now perform these tasks without consciously thinking about them.

Your subconscious mind learned to perform these tasks because you performed them repeatedly with your conscious mind. One of the programming keys to the subconscious mind is repetition.

Mind traps

Mind traps are often called 'thinking errors,' 'negative automatic thoughts,' and 'unhelpful ideas' because they are frequently erroneous, critical, or unhelpful. Mind traps can absorb your thoughts, including what you focus on, and influence your emotions, decisionmaking, and behaviors. You can fall into mental traps anytime, but you are more prone to do so under stress. If you feel as though your mind has gotten away from you or is "spiraling," there's a good possibility you're in a mental trap. Awareness of common thought traps is an essential first step in cultivating mindfulness. Some traps will lure you into the future, while others may ensnare you in the past.

- Catastrophizing
- Making hasty decisions
- Tunnel thinking
- The confirmation trap
- The conformity trap
- The sunk costs trap
- The blame trap

1. **Catastrophizing:** torturing oneself with unsettling ideas about potential future outcomes

15

and worst-case situations. For instance, if you know you must go somewhere new, you anticipate getting lost. If you have a mole on your skin that you're confident will turn out to be malignant melanoma, if your boss didn't look at you during a meeting, or if you believe you're about to be fired. Worry can be a healthy reaction that keeps you from acting recklessly or a catalyst for action that motivates you to take charge of a circumstance.

For instance, you might take a map and the Sat Nav with you on that trip; after the meeting, you might ask your boss if there's a problem; or you might schedule an appointment with your doctor to examine that mole. You can worry about things you have little control over, such as your dread of flying, being involved in a terrorist attack, or being robbed, in addition to things you can manage.

Worrying strengthens those brain pathways and makes that way of thinking your default mode as you mentally replay the worst-case scenario more and more. You are letting unfavorable scenarios for the future rule what is occurring right now.

2.   Jumping to conclusions: Judging or making a decision before you have all the necessary knowledge or have considered the available facts.

At a meeting, you are introduced to Joel. He gives off the impression of being a shy man. You know that he is either a librarian or an estate agent. Which one do you believe he is most likely? Were you tempted to think he's a librarian? Is that because you associate estate agents with extroverted personalities?

Jumping to conclusions is tough to avoid because our brains are geared for speed. It is more difficult to understand what is going on when you maintain an open mind. How will you know when you've seen everything there is to see? How long should you wait while keeping an open mind? Keep in mind that your brain frequently takes shortcuts without your awareness. But when you make a hasty judgment, you rely on past information or experience to know what will happen in the future.

3.   Tunnel thinking: Imagine looking down a cardboard tube. What do you observe? More importantly, what can't you see? Your mind eliminates options and possibilities when you think in a tunnel, thus the name.

There is one direction to go: down and out of the tunnel. This is helpful in a crisis when you need to concentrate your attention and disregard irrelevant or unneeded information. But what sights and attractions are you missing if, for instance, you drive someplace and only concentrate on getting there, on the destination? In the grand scheme, missing out on the landscape and exciting sites is not bad.

On the other hand, what if a detective investigating a suspect in a crime, or a doctor seeking to identify a health issue, narrowed their focus instead of evaluating all alternatives and evidence? Future-dependent happiness and tunnel thinking are related; for some, there is never enough. Do you say things like, "I'll be happy when I find a partner" or "I'll be happy when I acquire a new job"? Perhaps you feel that the house you live in or your garden isn't what you desire, and you long for a bigger and better place. Such a focus can help you work towards a goal.

However, it may keep you from being attentive because you are overly preoccupied with the future and neglect the present moment, your surroundings, and your feelings and experiences. You miss out on happiness now when you concentrate your happiness on something in the future. You could find it difficult to accept that a relationship didn't work out. Or perhaps you failed to land that position or position on a course some time ago, and if only you had, your life would be much better. You're mired in the past, and it's taking up your present.

4. **The confirmation trap:** is when you seek information to validate your preconceived notions. Consider this situation: Paul, who has lately experienced mental health issues, should not be included in the team that will be working on the new project, in Lauren's opinion. Lauren calls a coworker who has also excluded Paul to be sure; she hopes that he will support her reasoning. Lauren has already made a decision (based on the past).

She is seeking information that will confirm her current beliefs while avoiding anything that contradicts them. It turns out that Paul had a breakdown in this case 18 months ago and is now fully healed.

Making decisions based on experience might be helpful, but it is not always beneficial. The confirmation trap keeps you from being conscious because you risk being misled by outdated ideas or knowledge and unable to see things in light of the most recent information. Remember that the confirmation trap can also serve as the foundation for prejudice, which is the act of prejudging a circumstance or a person based on a preconceived attitude or sentiment developed beforehand without adequate justification or knowledge.

5. **The conformity trap:** falling in with other people's way of thinking. Do you know the story of the emperor's new clothes?

The emperor enjoyed dressing up in stylish attire and parading across his realm so that people may admire him. Two thugs once boasted to the emperor that they were skilled tailors and could make him a gorgeous new suit. It would appear invisible since it would be so light and delicate. Only those who were stupid could not see it.

 The emperor, who was ecstatic, gave the order for the "tailors" to start working. Eventually, the emperor's new suit was ready. Although he was blind, he did not want to appear an idiot. He admired the suit and thanked the tailors.
He marched along the street so that everyone could see his new attire. The only thing the populace could see was a naked emperor, but no one said anything out of fear of appearing foolish. They foolishly praised the invisible fabric and the colors. The emperor was delighted. At last, a child cried, "The emperor is naked!" Everyone quickly started muttering the same thing, and soon they were all yelling, "The emperor is not wearing anything!"

For most of us, questioning what we are told feels rude and intrusive.

Additionally, because we are chastised for challenging authority, we repress the inclination to challenge our assumptions. To a greater or lesser extent, we accept other people's views and ways of thinking, even when they lead to harmful or destructive thoughts and behaviors. Adhering to the opinions of others can indeed facilitate social interactions. Still, it's also simple to get caught up in a single interpretation of the world and only to view things from one point of view.

6.   The sunk costs trap: the time and effort you have already put into a situation and can never get back. Sunk costs can deceive you into continuing something you would be better off terminating, leading you to invest more time, energy, or money in someone or something even when it is not helping you. Maybe you're in a new job but hate it, making you miserable.

However, due to the sacrifices you made in your life to be able to accept the new job—you left home, for example—you refuse to give up, believing that "I messed up." It's too late to turn back at this point, so move on with the expectation that things will improve. You can't abandon your goals too quickly; otherwise, nothing will get done. But if you can't let go, you're letting the past rule the present rather than realizing that only what happens going forward matters.

7.   **The blame trap:** putting the entire blame for a mistake on someone or something else. Here's what happened to Melinda: "I had already traveled a few miles outside of town when I came across it; the gas gauge's red light indicated that I was almost out of gas.

For miles, there was not a single service station. My husband came to mind next. "Why does he always drive it until it's almost empty? Why didn't he fill up the car when he drove it last night? He knew I was going to need it today. He's so thoughtless. Why does this always happen to me?" And there she was, in the midst of the blame game.

How frequently do you react like this, looking for someone to blame for your awful circumstance? The blame trap offers no advantages. There's frequently nothing you can do to change anything once it's happened. But because you are reluctant to accept what has occurred, you are also unable to concentrate on and control the current situation.

You're caught up in the blame game! Like all traps, mind traps catch you unawares and are difficult to escape from. People tend to be mindless often; they are oblivious when in that state of mind since they are "not there" to notice. But if you're aware of them, you'll see that they're not insurmountably challenging to get out of. Just being aware of mind traps is mindful. You can escape a thought trap as soon as you become aware that you are in one.

Was what you were doing on your mind? There is no need to categorize your thoughts as good, terrible, or incorrect; categorizing your thoughts is another mind trap. Developing the ability to be more present with these mind traps is the first step to breaking free from them.

Identify your feelings

All mind traps —blaming others, jumping to conclusions and tunnel thinking. come with emotions, such as worry, anxiety, anger, guilt and fear. How are emotions linked to being mindful? Let's start with defining emotions. Most people would say that emotions and feelings are the same things. In actuality, sentiments are only one component of emotion.

Any emotion has three components: thoughts, behavior, and feelings. Emotions result from the interaction between these ideas, actions, and bodily sensations. The behavioral side of emotion is its outward manifestation or the things you do or don't do when you're feeling it. If, for instance, you are concerned about losing your work, you might speak with your trade union or start making arrangements to launch your own business. On the other hand, your anxiety could render you helpless to the point where you accomplish nothing!

Cognitive aspect

This aspect of emotion involves your thoughts. It is the internal, conscious, and subjective component of emotion. If you were concerned about losing your job, you could have concluded, "I'll never get another employment." Or they could say, "Great, I'll retrain and do something different."

Physical aspect

This element of emotion refers to the physical modifications an emotion causes in your body. Your body releases adrenaline when you are anxious, worried, or excited. Your body releases serotonin when you're calm and content. Therefore, depending on how you think about the prospect of losing your job, your body will respond physically in a different way. Aspects of emotion can occur in any order, yet each can impact the others. For instance, your thoughts might influence how you feel physically.

It can also alter how you behave. But it's also true that your actions can alter your thoughts, affecting how you feel physically.

Being mindful of your emotions

 The next time you feel an emotion, whether anger, excitement, guilt, or pride, attempt to break it down into all of its component pieces. Starting with any physical cues or sensations, ask yourself where they seem to be coming from.

These physiological changes—increased heart rate, a hot flash, sweat, muscle strain, stomach knots, and shivering—intensify the mood. You can learn to be aware of these signs with a bit of practice. Next, observe your thoughts. What goes in your mind, for example, when feeling guilty? When you are feeling grateful, what are your thoughts? Finally, be aware of how you behave.

What don't you do?

What do you do?

What actions do you take?

Just doing this exercise in itself is being mindful.

It not only makes you more conscious of your feelings but also enables you to see how your emotions are connected, how they interact, and how they affect you. The more conscious you are of your emotions, the easier it will be to break free of thought patterns or automatic responses.

All emotions are positive.

It's easy to think of emotions as either positive or negative. Every emotion has a beneficial intention that promotes physical and interpersonal wellbeing.

Physical safety value of emotions

First and foremost, emotions shield you and keep you secure. Your emotions facilitate your ability to react fast when rational thought is too slow. It would help if you reacted fast in a potentially harmful scenario and feelings like fear and surprise aid in that process.

The social importance of emotions

Social emotions, such as love, trust, and gratitude, help you feel emotionally tied to other people and welcomed, needed and cared for. They also help you feel like you belong. To experience being recognized, valued, encouraged, and, if necessary, forgiven. Feelings of guilt, shame, humiliation, and pride encourage you to examine and modify your behavior and interpersonal interactions. For instance, trust motivates sharing and cooperation. You do something you should or shouldn't have done because you feel guilty.

Clutter of the mind

Numerous individuals suffer from having "too much on their minds." You may be concerned about the future, ruminating on regrets from the past, or fussing over a lengthy mental to-do list. When your mind is filled with a multitude of thoughts, it is tough to concentrate and be productive. Everything can appear overwhelming, which frequently induces worry or panic.

When our minds are cluttered with many thoughts, it becomes challenging to concentrate and process information. Imagine a fish pond overrun with weeds and invasive predators; the pond's output will be drastically diminished. A cluttered mind is disruptive and detrimental to productivity, equilibrium, and mental wellness. You forget important dates, feel pushed in several directions, and cannot complete a project or assignment from start to finish.

Do you glance about your home and wonder how it became so cluttered with knickknacks, or survey your office and wonder how it became buried in unused stacks of paper? Is your calendar brimming with appointments that extend indefinitely into the future? Your inbox is so full that you don't even feel like diving in to address anything but the most urgent matters. All of this physical and mental clutter can impede your flow in terms of mobility and cognition. It turns out that your well-being may also be affected by the so-called "clutter effect." Recent research on stress, life happiness, physical health, and cognition all demonstrate the need for simplifying.

Many people's first association with clutter is the interior of a hoarder's residence. However, cluttering may involve collecting more items than the available area can accommodate. All of the artifacts scattered throughout the rooms of a 25-room home will fit comfortably on shelves and tables. The amount of belongings in a tight two-bedroom flat is an entirely different problem.

Why clutter is bad for your brain

It may appear harmless to have overflowing cabinets and stacks of paper throughout the home. However, evidence indicates that disorder and chaos have a cumulative effect on our minds. Constant visual reminders of disorganization deplete our cognitive resources, decreasing our concentration capacity. Visual clutter contributes to cognitive overload and can impair our working memory.

In 2011, neuroscientists utilizing fMRI (functional magnetic resonance imaging) and other physiological measurements discovered that decluttering the home and workplace led to improved concentration and information processing and higher productivity.

Clutter can induce stress, anxiety, and depression. A chronically cluttered home environment might induce a continual, low-grade fight-or-flight response, exhausting our survival resources. This response can cause psychological changes that impact our ability to fight off pathogens, digest food, and increase our risk for type 2 diabetes and cardiovascular disease. Additionally, clutter may have ramifications for our relationships with others. A 2016 U.S. study, for instance, indicated that participants were less able to correctly understand the facial emotions of movie characters when the background was cluttered.

Surprisingly, it does not disappear when we eventually retire to bed. People who sleep in messy rooms are more likely to experience sleep issues, such as trouble falling asleep and nighttime disruptions.

Clutter can generate or exacerbate stress levels. This stress is capable of causing both physical and mental disorders. Stress can muddle the mind, making it difficult to focus and concentrate. As a result of the accumulation of filth and germs, disorder and filth can also induce illness. Sickness can make it difficult to think clearly and be productive. A chaotic and cluttered residence might make it uncomfortable to spend time there. This is unhealthy, as one's house should be a sanctuary where one can unwind and enjoy themselves. This relaxation and delight can be directly opposed by a congested atmosphere. Clutter caused by disorganization and lack of order can make it difficult (if not impossible) to locate items, increasing tension and anger.

This irritating mental fog is becoming more prevalent in our increasingly busy and interconnected society. We can clean our minds and prevent unnecessary brain drain with a few minor adjustments to our routine and habits. Decluttering your home can unleash positive energy, providing vitality, health, and the ability to experience the highest level of relaxation and bringing tranquility and harmony to your house. Once you have gotten rid of the clutter, you can concentrate and find what you need when you need it. It may be pretty liberating. If you are hesitant, choose any room and complete the process; you will feel a tremendous weight lifted from your shoulders. You will realize that the space is energizing and makes you feel fantastic.

So, if you are feeling weighed down by constant mind-chatter and clutter, try these six simple tips to help regain your focus:

1. Keep a journal

Journaling is a terrific method to organize your ideas and clear your mind. According to research, expressive writing reduces unpleasant event-related intrusive thoughts and enhances working memory. It frees your mind and helps you to manage worry and stress more effectively. Keeping a journal is an excellent way to manage mental clutter and provides a space to analyze and clarify one's mind.

2. Let go of the past

Many individuals experience clutter due to clinging to the past or fixating on events beyond their control. It is crucial to learn how to let go of the things you cannot alter, whether dwelling on past mistakes or being weighed down by what others think of you. This will not only improve your mental health and help you to be more present, but it will also reduce unneeded concerns and ideas.

3. Limit your notifications

We are more interconnected than ever. While this positively affects our professional and social life, the frequent notifications we get from social media, messaging apps, emails, and other sources can often be a mental drain. According to a study, receiving a push notification is as distracting as responding to a text message or phone call. Limiting the alerts, you receive on your desktop and mobile devices will allow you to concentrate better and have fewer mental distractions.

4. Meditate

Meditation is an effective method for clearing the mind and enhancing focus. A study that examined the effects of an eight-week mindfulness meditation course discovered that mindful meditation enhanced participant's ability to reorient and retain their attention. By prioritizing meditation in your daily routine, you enable yourself to declutter your mind and retain focus every day.

5. Keep a list

It can feel like we have an unending amount of everyday tasks. Avoid overwhelming by keeping a list of your daily tasks and prioritizing them according to timeliness and importance. While there are several online tools that you can use to make your daily list, one of the most effective ways is simply jotting it down with pen and paper. Research shows that our brains process abstract information more effectively when we read it on paper. So, grab a pen and pad, write down the essential task of the day, and determine how you will fit these around meetings, calls, and lunch breaks.

6. Embrace a routine

A daily routine ensures that you can start the day off right and creates an overall sense of stability in your life. It enables you to maintain efficiency and instills good habits, such as healthy decision-making, exercising, and getting enough sleep, reducing mental clutter.

Any mental clutter can hinder performance and undermine mental wellness. Cleaning your thoughts and decluttering may infuse your daily life with productivity, concentration, and, most importantly, peace.

Stress and the Mind

Stress can signify different things to different people. For instance, if you were an engineering student and mentioned the word "stress," you would be referring to a force sufficient to bend or distort a system. Webster's definition of stress is as follows: Stress is a bodily reaction to stimuli, such as fear or pain, that upsets or interferes with average psychological balance; it is also referred to as strain or tension and can be physical or mental, or emotional.

Now the "stress" we are accustomed to hearing about is the "stress" that is capable of causing mood swings, bodily ailments, and addictions, as well as giving you the reflexes to avoid a drunk driver while also allowing you to enjoy the fantastic pleasures that happen in the bedroom. People frequently discuss stress, yet few have a deep understanding of it.

The Canadian endocrinologist Dr. Hans Selye coined the contemporary definition of "stress" as the wear and tear of a fast-paced lifestyle. Due to his research and discoveries in this field, Dr. Hans Selye is frequently referred to as the "father of stress." Dr. Selye found a well-known series of psychological changes that occur anytime a person is subjected to excessive pressure or is confronted with severe obstacles. He referred to these alterations as the "stress reaction," nonspecific response of the body to any pressure placed upon it, whether emotional, physical, or mental.

Stress was never intended to be present at all times. According to Robert Sapolsky, a professor at Stanford, you are only supposed to feel stressed during the final five minutes of your life. When a wild animal is chasing you through the savanna, your stress reaction is designed to save your life by mobilizing your attention, muscles, and immune system to get you out of danger as quickly as possible. When animals escape, they immediately transition from "fight-or-flight" mode to "rest-and-digest" mode, where their parasympathetic nervous system replenishes their supplies. This stress response is intended to be brief because it depletes your body, health, and vitality. It also affects your emotional intelligence and decision-making skills. When you are tense, you are more prone to react to situations rather than reply rationally.

You interpret the world differently as well. We become myopic due to stress, preventing us from seeing the broader picture. When we are more relaxed, our focus expands. We perceive more things. In one study, participants received a three-month training in meditation. The participants next performed an attentional blink task, in which images emerged rapidly. Typically, people's attention does not pick up all of the target images during this activity. Participants could recognize more of the target images following mindfulness training, indicating that their mental state had become more attentive.

Attending more events allows you to observe more about other people and converse with them more effectively. High levels of stress and anxiety (or any bad feeling) cause us to focus on ourselves for an evolutionary reason. When our ancestors were anxious, they were in a survival dilemma. It was beneficial to concentrate on oneself to save your own life.

Most people feel that the power of the mind is a person's most significant potential; thus, the widespread expression "Mind over Matter." As an illustration, you have a headache but ignore it, believing it will pass - and occasionally, it does. Undeniably, you are not the only person who believes in this ability; millions, if not billions, of individuals across the globe, have this belief. Stress is something that every person on the planet experiences. There is a relation between the mind and the body, similar to what the Austro-Hungarian Hans Selye, MD, Ph.D. discovered and wrote in his book The Stress of Life; it's the same as when you're stressed, and you have migraines, ulcers, insomnia, and occasionally even cancer. Why do these occurrences occur? It is the power of the mind; our mind can make us sick and well. As described by Dr. Selye, these stress hormones can damage our immunological, muscular, skeletal, and many other organs and systems. You believe that you are under stress, which causes your body to manufacture these so-called stress hormones that go throughout your entire system and alter them.

Consequently, you feel awful. On the other hand, when you believe that you will recover, that it will pass, and that you will feel better, you will recover. Similar to persons who undergo numerous trials, one group is given a medicine that, for example, reduces stress, and the other group is given a placebo. Occasionally, even the placebo group will claim that they have experienced improvements in their stress levels; however, they were only taking placebos.

In truth, the mind can help you feel better and make you sick. Similar to Emile Coue's autosuggestion, "Day by day in every way, I am getting better and better," it is evident that the power of the mind ostensibly tells the body that it will get better; the mind-body medicine. Coue's treatment consisted of instructing his patients to repeat this famous phrase twice daily. He firmly felt that it is preferable to focus on the positive outcomes you desire rather than the unfavorable ones. When you wish to get cured, imagine that you will be well; do not think that you don't feel well since your mind and body will believe this, and you will consequently feel poorly. You will have a greater chance of leading a more positive and enjoyable life if you continue to concentrate on and visualize the positive things.

When under stress, we are less likely to notice if a colleague appears exhausted or depressed and more likely to become upset if they do not meet our expectations. Nevertheless, when you are calmer and happier, you will likely have more empathy: You will take the time to reach out to your colleague and see if there is anything you can do to assist them. When you're calm, you regulate your energy since you're not continually expending it by spending your days in sympathetic nervous system overdrive. Calm allows you to concentrate on your tasks and do them much more swiftly. Also, tranquility can affect your creativity. According to research, our most creative thoughts occur when we are not actively concentrated or worried. We are creative when relaxed and in alpha wave mode, such as having a shower or walking in the woods. Those who attend a four-day immersion nature retreat return with a 50 percent increase in creativity do to having a calm mind.

Change your mind

Your mind is incredible! It can rationalize, reason, think and understand. It observes, evaluates, and adjudicates. It can empathize and sympathize. It controls your willpower, intentions, decisions, and choices. Your mind can plan, fantasize, dream and anticipate. It can worry, misremember, and lie. Research has shown that mindfulness can alter the physical structure of our brains. According to brain scans, people who consistently practice mindfulness have thicker areas of the brain that are responsible for processing sensory information and paying attention. The thickening is more apparent in older individuals than in younger ones in one region of the grey matter. According to study leader Sara Lazar, a psychologist at Harvard Medical School, "our data imply that meditation practice can improve cortical plasticity in adults in areas essential for cognitive and emotional processing and well-being."
"A mature brain's structure can alter in response to repeated practice."

Aside from degenerative brain disorders, your brain is effectively malleable and continuously rewiring itself, so it never loses its capacity for learning and change. The "magic" of mindfulness changes how brain networks are organized. The fascinating part is that you have control over this talent; you can tell your brain to use itself to make things! Your brain is divided into three primary regions that evolved during human evolution: the limbic brain, the neocortex, and the reptile brain.

Each has an important role. Your limbic and reptile brains intuitively respond to the environment around you, devoid of conscious thought or reasoning. In actuality, limbic reactions are hard-wired into your body, making it challenging to conceal them. (Try suppressing a startled response when something makes you jump.) Limbic responses are reflections of your attitudes, feelings, and intentions.

Your mind might get overrun by emotions like fear, shame, rage, and excitement. The neo-cortex, the new brain, controls your cognitive functions, including thinking, remembering, and reasoning. Focus and attention are primary activities of the neocortex.

Focused attention calms irrelevant limbic brain activity when practicing mindfulness. Your mind becomes quieter. Remember, any thought or action creates a neural pathway in the brain. When you make a particular thinking style a habit, it becomes your default position. Therefore, the more you think or act in a particular manner, and the more often you follow that path, the more probable it is to happen again. The good news is that you can replace destructive thought patterns with productive ones by repeatedly going through the same procedure. You eventually developed a method of thinking and acting, and those ways of thinking and acting eventually became automatic. It results naturally from the way your brain functions. Whatever method you select, you may make the most of this process to create and establish fresh paradigms for thinking and acting. Although leopards can't alter their spots, you can because you're not a leopard. You can learn to think in a more open, flexible way.

RIPPLES: THOUGHTS

Every thought we have determines our future. -
Louise Hay.

Imagine an utterly motionless pond with no signs of a wave or even a ripple. The pond is tranquil, but when you toss a rock at it, you can see that the stone's splash causes ripples that grow into waves, disrupting the pond's tranquility until the splash's effect vanishes. Now visualize your thoughts. The mind is tranquil and still in its standard form, just like a pond. However, when you start thinking in a certain way, a sequence of thoughts begins to ripple outward and occupy your thoughts until they stop or until you learn to manage your thinking pattern.

Every thought you have has the same ability to cause waves as throwing a rock into a pool of water. We employ only a tiny portion of our remarkable intellect daily, as you have undoubtedly heard. The balance of positive and negative thoughts we carry can provide the groundwork for many things in our lives, both good and bad. Our ideas have a significant impact on how we see the world.

Despair or insecurity are frequent causes of negativity. It might emerge as a result of illness, experiences in life, conflicts in personality, or drug addiction. Negativity may become a habit, just like many other things in life. Regular denial, cynicism, and criticism can help the brain create neural circuits that encourage sadness. The facts may be distorted due to these adverse tendencies, making it much harder to stop the downward spiral.

Stress levels are usually correlated with negative thoughts. Insomnia, an elevated heart rate, hypertension, eating disorders, substance addiction, alcoholism, memory issues, outbursts of fury, anxiety, or other potentially serious health issues are all linked to elevated stress. You can categorically consider yourself ill. Additionally, by disrupting the hormone balance in our body and altering the neurotransmitters in the brain, negative attitudes further erode our sense of wellbeing.

A negative thought is an interior dialogue that encourages self-hatred, self-blame and ruminating. It ridicules, humiliates, terrifies, and seduces us into engaging in self-destructive or self-limiting behavior. It warns us not to depend too heavily on the people we care about. It affects whether we give up on a goal.

This idea permeates each of us in some manner. Maybe yours is more focused on your career.

"Accept your current position rather than going after that promotion. You are not a successful person." Perhaps it's giving you dating advice "not go on dates. It has no use. No one will ever love you. You must spend your time alone." Like many people, you probably have a confident, upbeat, and self-compassionate side, but you also have conflicting emotions. And although one is life-affirming and goal-oriented, the other is negative toward oneself, hates oneself, and finally destroys oneself.

Be wary of voices that seem paranoid or conceited about other people. "Nobody sees the potential in you. They don't value you at all. Simply put, they are jealous of you." Although these ways of thinking may seem sympathetic or even encouraging, they frequently leave you feeling empty and divert you from your objectives.

In addition, once you act on these beliefs, more serious self-attacks are in store for you. "There you are again, all by yourself. What an idiot!"
It is better to stop thinking and instead act in a way that is contrary to your thoughts when you realize that you are overthinking and that they are damaging. Resisting the influence of these voices on your behavior is a part of zero-tolerance. Invite a friend over for coffee if they encourage you to

spend some time alone. Apply for that senior position if they are denigrating your professional successes. You can anticipate your voices being louder when you first change how you look. However, your actions become more restrained the longer you continue them. It's challenging to judge yourself for being slothful when you exercise regularly and actively seek your goals.

How our thoughts can alter reality.

"If you have a peaceful mind and thoughts, water becomes more peaceful." – **Dr. Emoto**.

Thoughts have no force in and of themselves; only when we actively engage our attention in them do they become real. And when we interact with particular thoughts, we begin to feel the feelings that these thoughts elicit, and we enter a new emotional state that drives our behavior.

If you routinely engage with the notion that you are a failure and give it more attention, you may begin to feel discouraged, worthless, disheartened, and possibly depressed. How does this affect your body? You sulk, hunch your shoulders, and lack self-assurance. But engage in more empowering thoughts. They will enhance your confidence and elicit a more positive emotional state, reflecting how your body reacts: standing tall, being cheery, and feeling invigorated. The frequency of vibration of these emotions then flows back into the originating thought process. And while we continue to pay mental attention to the initial thought, the feeling is reaffirmed, thereby energizing the thinking.

Dr. Masaru Emoto Water experiment.

We are reflected in the water. Some claim that Dr. Masaru Emoto created the groundbreaking yet natural concept that water directly reflects human words and ideas. Masaru Emoto (1943–2014) was a Japanese scientist who devoted his life to studying the "language" of water. He made a crucial discovery: water has a memory and can store information. The significant part of this discovery is that water reacts differently according to the information it gets, displaying through its crystals patterns that can be more or less harmonic. These experiments showed human thoughts and intentions could physically alter the molecular structure of water. Specifically, the water crystals were altered simply through conscious intention.

During his research, Emoto split water into a hundred Petri dishes and assigned each Petri dish a positive or negative outcome. The good water was blessed or praised for its greatness, while the bad water was reprimanded. Allegedly, each petri dish was frozen under identical conditions. When the frozen water was examined under a microscope, it was discovered that the praised and valued water had rearranged itself into magnificent crystalline patterns. The "poor" water was as unattractive as ice crystals, lacking symmetry and generally jagged.

Remember that you are composed of about 70% water and that the water in your body acts precisely as described above. However, the people around you are also comprised of water! This idea explains how your words, thoughts, and emotions can affect and alter the person or living organism to whom they are addressed (Animals and food).

Dr. Emoto demonstrated that words have a vibration and will alter the structure of water crystals. He found that uplifting, positive, and encouraging words created beautiful, balanced, and symmetric crystals. Destructive, hateful, and evil words had the opposite effect on the water crystals. The research clearly shows how the power of positivity can transform anything in our physical reality.

When we are uncomfortable with our current situation in life, we want to effect change. Therefore, we transform our environment believing that doing so would produce the desired transformation. We purchase items for a boost of materialistic bliss. We travel to escape our difficulties. We search for substances that dull the mind and aid in forgetting. Nevertheless, we inevitably return to where we began: dissatisfied with where we are now. Thus, the cycle continues to perpetuate. We shop, travel, and forget to always concentrate on the external variables that must be modified to improve our circumstances. This occurs because we incorrectly believe that change originates from the outside. In reality, the environment plays a part in altering your circumstances, but it does not address the underlying cause (your thinking) that is the driving force behind your feelings.

Here's what you need to realize:

If you wish to alter the outer, you must first alter the inner. It would help if you altered the focus of your thoughts because what you think directly affects how you feel, how you feel immediately affects how your body reacts, how your body reacts directly affects how you conduct, and how you behave ultimately defines who you are and what you encounter in life.

Every thought we have causes a chemical reaction in the brain, which triggers an emotion. This thinking establishes a new circuit that sends a signal to the body, causing a specific response. The more we practice this pattern, the more it becomes ingrained in our minds and a habit.

Thought Journal

Writing down one's thoughts is one approach to begin becoming more self-aware. Include shopping, cooking, driving to work or picking up the kids from school, reading a story to your child, watching television, attending a meeting, sending an email, gardening, and indulging in physical activity among your recent 24 hours activities.

Where was your thought? At the current moment? Or ruminating on the past or rushing into the future?

Every day, a variety of incidents were documented. Things such as my manager passing me in the hallway without a word (she must be mad since I disagreed with her in the meeting yesterday). I ignored her news since I was too worried about what I had to do when I came home to attend a coffee date with a friend. I'm eating a sandwich while continuing to work (I can't stop for lunch). Evening commitment to organize my daughter's Brownie meeting (why did I agree to do this every Tuesday night?).

Keeping track of my ideas helped me recognize trends in my mind processes. I was astounded at the frequency with which I allowed past and future thoughts to interfere with the present. Although writing everything down may seem like a lot of work, it makes the exercise more successful. This is because it heightens your awareness before and throughout the writing process.

Ask yourself periodically throughout the day, "Do I know where my mind is?" You could also try:
The alarm on your phone can be set to sound frequently throughout the day at random intervals. Every time the alarm goes off, first become aware of it, then record your thoughts and actions at the time.

Emotions

Emotion is a remarkable yet widely misunderstood phenomenon. Everyone has them, experiences ups and downs from time to time, and at times is unable to identify the underlying emotion. Emotion is a mysterious, indefinable entity whose dictionary definition cannot describe: "a feeling that affects my mood." You may often have a feeling inappropriate to the circumstance, which can be perplexing.

Perhaps emotions come up without any trigger that you are aware of. Water is tasteless; it has no flavor. If the flavor is added, it can be coca cola, coffee, tea, sweet or sour, minerals, sugar, or salt; the taste depends entirely on what is added to the water, but the water itself is still tasteless. Your moods will alter in response to experiences that trigger thoughts via the identification process.

Feeling in and of itself is neutral; your thoughts guide your emotion, and you label it as positive or bad based on the thoughts you used to direct the emotion's energy. In reality, it is not feeling but your positive or negative thoughts that determine the direction of your emotions. Then, you experience something and refer to it as an emotion of that type. You add sugar or salt to water based on your perceptions of how you want the water to taste, sweet or salty. However, if you are not attentive and alert, and present, you could mistake salt for sugar. You want something sweet, but you obtain something salty because you are not paying attention to your thoughts. You feel, then let a specific notion enter your head, and your feeling is influenced by that thinking, even if it is contrary to what you would or should feel at the time.

Understanding that emotions are reactions to something that has occurred in the past or may occur in the future is another method to comprehend emotions. The emotion of disgust, for instance, can be a response to any current event. Despite being experienced in the present, thankfulness is a response to an event that occurred in the past, whether an hour, a day, a week or even years ago. Other responses to the past include regret, shame, and guilt. They can all influence your current thoughts and actions and offer you information. On the other hand, hope, optimism, and enthusiasm are present-moment emotions associated with future occurrences that will occur tomorrow, next week, or next month. The potential for the future also produces anxiety, fear, and rage. The emotions resulting from prospective future events have the same effect on your current thoughts and behaviors as those resulting from past ones.

When you reflect on a former experience, you enter the past and leave the present. The same holds while contemplating the future. Since emotions are always experienced in the present, they might be viewed as departures from it. Emotions are transient and fleeting. Mindfulness comes when you know emotion and what it is trying to communicate. Instead of letting our emotions lead and inform us, we frequently allow them to control us. This pulls us either into the past or into the future.

For example, sorrow is an internalized emotion characterized by emotions of helplessness and loss. Sadness has a purpose by causing individuals to slow down and cope with loss. However, melancholy becomes problematic when it leads to a downward spiral that might lead to depression. When unexpectedly placed in dangerous situations, terror helps you choose between flight and combat. Fear can become a problem when you are constantly tense, fearful, and ready to fight or flee. Realizing you have done or are doing something wrong should push you to take urgent action to rectify the situation. When you are trapped in the past and cannot stop thinking about what you did or did not do, guilt becomes an issue. Therefore, emotions are intended to be quick messages that encourage you to take action. When emotions, however, dominate your thinking, you become locked in the present or the future.

How do you stop your emotions from trapping you in the past or future? You begin by acknowledging your emotions. To embrace your emotions, it is not required to analyze what, how, and why you feel the way you do. It merely requires acknowledging your sensations, regardless of their origin. Imagine you were just let down by a friend who abruptly canceled on you (again). You are resentful, dissatisfied, and feel taken advantage of. You are irritated that she "made" you feel this way. Do yourself a favor and accept your feelings rather than blaming your friend and telling yourself, "I've been disappointed. It's normal to feel unsatisfied and upset. It is acceptable for me to have these feelings.

Simply being aware of and recognizing a feeling can prevent its dominance. Be vigilant to prevent this; you return to the present by being aware of and embracing your thoughts and emotions. Accepting an emotion allows it to exist without seeking to change the sensation, incident, or experience that triggered it. Regardless of how you feel, acceptance relieves you of unnecessary misery. What it is, it is.

The next time you experience an emotion, whether it be rage, excitement, guilt, or pride, try to dissect it into its parts. Ask yourself, beginning with any physical clues or sensations, where they seem to originate. These physiological changes—increased heart rate, a hot flash, perspiration, muscle tension, knots in the stomach, and shivering—intensify the mood. You can learn to recognize these indicators with a bit of practice. Observe your thoughts; what do you think about, for instance, when feeling guilty? What are your thoughts when you experience gratitude?

Finally, be conscious of your behavior; what should you avoid doing? What do you do? Which acts do you perform? This exercise in and of itself demonstrates mindfulness. It not only makes you more aware of your emotions but also enables you to recognize how they are related, how they affect you, and how they interact. The greater your awareness of your emotions, the simpler it will be to break away from habitual thought patterns or automatic responses.

BUBBLES: LIMITING BELIEFS

"If you adopt a limiting thought, it will become your reality." —**Louise Hay.**

I was walking around the pond one day; there was no disturbance with the pond, and the weather was calm, but I could see bubbles pop up inside the pond once in a while. Bubbles are like Past Trauma, fears, and negative beliefs that keep returning to your mind anytime you want to do something related to your experience. It might be in a new business you want to start or a relationship.

Have you ever questioned what prevents you from achieving your dreams of a beautiful relationship, the ideal job, and financial freedom? Your limiting thoughts are preventing you from achieving the results you desire. These ideas frequently stem from a place of negativity and fear, which prevents us from taking advantage of new chances.

Allow me to pose the following question:

- When you describe yourself, what are the most common things you tell people you always/never do?

- In what areas of your life would you like to have more confidence?
- Which motivational quotes make you want to yell "B.S.!" every time you hear them?

A limiting belief is a mental state or self-perception that confines you in some way. These beliefs are frequently untrue statements you create about yourself, which can have various harmful consequences. Limiting beliefs are assumptions we make about ourselves, others, and the inaccurate world. They are limited because if we were to alter them, our life experience would begin to shift magically toward a much healthier, happier, and more fulfilling lifestyle.

Several examples that you may have heard or may have considered include the following:

- "I am unlovable."
- "I'm not smart, beautiful, or talented enough."
- "I'd never be able to start my own business."
- "I lack the necessary time, experience, and resources to pursue my interest."
- "At all costs, I should avoid failing."
- "I should never put authority in jeopardy."

- "I am too old to return to graduate school.
- "I'm divorced, and no one will want to date me."
- "It is too late to change my lifestyle."
- "At the end of the day, all romantic relationships end in heartbreak."

When you have a belief, it is as if it is fixed in stone, and you will seek proof to support it at every opportunity. Suppose you believe you are not destined to enjoy the more excellent things in life and that every dollar you make must be earned through the sweat of your labor. In that case, you will no doubt find an unending supply of examples to support your idea, further solidifying it.

On the other hand, if you believe that money comes readily and effortlessly to you, you will find proof to support that idea. It reverts to its original emphasis. Humans are creatures of elimination; we focus on what is essential and discard the rest. As a result, you cannot alter your concentration without first altering your beliefs. Identifying your "below the surface" limiting beliefs can be challenging, as they are frequently well protected by your subconscious mind, which is quite pleased to keep you in your comfort zone. However, to move forward, you must leave your comfort zone and be aware of your limiting thoughts.

Why is it essential to cut off limiting beliefs?

Limiting beliefs act as mental impediments to us reaching our goals and manifesting the reality we seek. Having these negative beliefs can harm all parts of your life, including the following:

- Career/Success
- Interactions between spouses/interpersonal interactions
- Money and finance
- Parenting
- Spirituality
- Mental and physical health

When we set limits in any of these areas, we will never realize our full potential of them.
Overcoming self-limiting ideas requires consistent, deliberate work. To keep them at bay, the same level of intentionality is required. Spend some time noticing and dealing with beliefs that come up repeatedly and new ones.

The Scarcity Mindset

The default setting ingrained in most humanity seems deeply rooted in lack and hardship. Many of us are mentally, emotionally, spiritually, and physically living in a place of such great struggle that even when a brilliant opportunity shows up, we cannot see or cease it to our benefit. There's a very debilitating idea running in the background of many people, carrying this belief that life is a struggle and things always have to be complicated. So when something extraordinary comes along, this belief in hardship prevents them from taking the necessary action or even considering some new risks because, in their minds, they've already settled on a "hard" and adverse outcome.

Suppose we have chosen to live life from this awareness. In that case, it's going to be hard to produce the desired results because new results require new methods and approaches, yet how can we embark on something new with the right attitude if we already believe that it's going to be complicated or that it might not work out? The irony of such a belief is that life never fails to prove us right. This is a classic case of scarcity thinking running a person's mind, which means their entire life and financial decisions will work to reflect the same. Scarcity thinking certainly sabotages your success and ability to create personal or professional breakthroughs. Whenever you find a team with a long losing history, even when they have a chance to secure a new victory, the old patterns seem to kick in, and they fall short yet again. It's tough to break the cycle of losing; in the same way, it's tough to break the cycle of winning hence the common saying that the rich get richer and the poor get poorer. But does this also apply in your life?

Your life conditions are all subject to the thought patterns running in your mind's background. We all operate based on our paradigms, and although paradigms are excellent and necessary, they can become our worst enemies when neglected or not upgraded over time.

Breaking the Scarcity Mindset

If you haven't been actively renewing your mind, likely, the current paradigms you have around the most critical subject relative to your life are all limited and outdated.

We waste time discussing the problems we want to overcome in life, describing them in detail, dissecting them, trying to figure out where they came from, and sometimes even talking down at those who conditioned us into said beliefs. This is just adding injury to the wound and doesn't resolve anything. Those who influenced you and gave you the current beliefs that keep you stuck only did the best they knew how with the awareness they had. Replaying old memories doesn't help you if your goal is to move forward and create more success in your life. My suggestion to you from now on is simply this:

- Find out if you have an active scarcity mindset (all you need to do is look around your life and the manifested conditions in your finances, health, relationships, work, and interaction with life). It won't be hard to figure out whether you live in the presence of abundance and prosperity or the absence of it. If still unsure, check out my list of the signs and symptoms of a scarcity mindset as I discuss this subject in greater detail.

- Take action immediately and learn how to renew and retrain your mind to be more tuned into abundance and prosperity. The mind's natural state is prosperity and abundance. Still, if it's been exposed to lack
for too long, some work must be done individually as soon as possible because

your mind determines the level of success you will enjoy.

There will always be many variables in the business world and life, but there's always going to be only one determining factor that makes or breaks the deal - you! A renewed mind is what breaks the scarcity paradigms and lack of consciousness.

- Let go of history and the need to blame others, issue judgment, or even victimize or hate on yourself once you discover that you dwell in awareness of lack and shortage.

  Going back to what I said before, it doesn't matter what happened in the past, whether it was wrong or right for society to believe so much in lack, for our parents to train us into scarcity awareness. All these things don't matter, the only thing that matters is what are you now willing and committed to doing to stop killing your efforts of success?

OVERCOMING LIMITING BELIEFS

By letting go of self-limiting beliefs and allowing your mind to soar to new heights- **Brian Tracy.**

Nobody disputes that creating goals is a necessary component of life transformation, whether primary, daring, or minor. While we have little difficulty outlining the objectives we wish to accomplish, putting these ideas into action is frequently more complicated than anticipated. A lack of self-control and motivation drives this behavior. However, other people are battling to improve their life for a lesser-known reason. It is due to their low self-efficacy. Individuals who lack self-efficacy struggle to form and implement strategies because they lack confidence in succeeding. You do not have to be aware that you exhibit typical behaviors associated with low self-efficacy for it to significantly impact your life.

What is the term "self-efficacy"?

Self-efficacy is the degree to which you believe you will carry out your tasks efficiently. It specifies such things as: - whether you continue or discontinue working on a particular mission; - how long you stay in the face of uncomfortable adjustments necessary to achieve long-term outcomes (diet, exercise regimens); - the objectives you set, and the line between "difficult" and "impossible." Your convictions about your abilities influence every aspect of your life. You are entirely in charge of your thoughts, feelings, and actions. You opt to write off activities that appear unreachable if you lack self-efficacy.

As a result, you will not think solely about achieving your goals; rather than reach your full potential, you will not live but just exist. It is critical to remember that self-efficacy is task related. You can develop high self-efficacy while driving a car and working in your business. However, high self-efficiency in some tasks implies increased self-effectiveness in other areas. In other words, high self-efficiency in one area of your life enables you to begin with the correct mindset in another.

Self-efficacy in general increases during adolescence. A good teacher will assist her students in developing a deep trust in the abilities that will empower them in adulthood. However, nothing is lost for those who did not establish a strong feeling of self-efficacy during their youth. Adults can acquire self-efficacy through various methods, which we will discuss in this chapter. Remove the past and think about what we can do in the present.

Five characteristics of individuals who have a strong sense of their effectiveness are as follows:

- They consider barriers as something to be overcome and mastered.

- They are tenacious in the face of adversity. They do not lose faith in their talents as a result of obstacles.

- You accept responsibility for your errors and feel you control the outcome (i.e., you do not believe in chance).

- They are making more sacrifices for a mission that enables them to do so.

- They stay focused on their objectives and gain a more nuanced understanding of how they can be accomplished.

- And here are five characteristics that people who are self-conscious about themselves share:

- Obstacles are avoided. As a result, they rarely (if ever) expand.

- They believe that lofty goals are beyond their capability and hence refrain from setting them, and they do not achieve tremendous successes.

- You quickly lose faith in your ability and give up on your aspirations.

- Rather than grasping core principles, they choose to scrutinize the surface and concentrate intently on the task at hand.

- You refuse to acknowledge that your actions and decisions affect your life (instead, they believe in external factors like luck).

I was a shy person with low self-efficacy; due to a great dread of death, developed by acquiring health difficulties in High school, I became an introverted person. Writing my children's books, I was asked to publicly speak at schools. All I could think was how am I supposed to do that? The day before I went to my first school, I shifted the way I thought about it. I changed my mind to think that if I inspired just one person it was worth it. I loved it so much I now publicly speak for a living.

The Galatean effect is a self-fulfilling prophecy that contributes significantly to our success. In exchange, inadequate self-efficiency might dramatically reduce one's prospects of personal success. If you don't trust your abilities, you're unlikely to establish lofty goals that will significantly improve your life. You do not provide your best (why would you invest in something that does not work?), and you also doubt your success ability. However, if you have a healthy sense of self-efficacy, you regularly raise the bar and improve yourself. Your career is an excellent area to look for this phenomenon. Individuals who lack confidence in their talents (despite possessing unique, valuable capabilities) are less likely to apply for and improve their positions as higher-paying employees. The option to grow a bakery franchise would be passed up by a small business owner who believes her bakery is the peak of her career. Her convictions either prevent her from acting or ultimately derail her efforts.

Apart from achievement, self-efficacy is most visible when it comes to health decisions. If you choose to smoke or quit, begin exercising three days a week, live a sedentary lifestyle, or gorge on junk food, your self-efficacy may change. Indeed, increasing your effectiveness is one of the most successful strategies for adhering to your practice strategy. Because individuals with low self-efficacy believe that numerous targets are not accomplished, they will never quit smoking. When faced with impediments to adjustment, low self-efficacy leads to a lack of commitment and little or no perseverance. People with a high level of self-efficacy can make a goal of quitting smoking entirely (and stick to it despite obstacles) (and give up when faced with the temptation to smoke more). Many people's weight loss may be due to a lack of self-efficacy, not only self-discipline. Because your self-efficacy level (confidence in your ability to lose weight) diminishes with each failure, you enter a vicious cycle that results in even more losses. You immediately abandon the goal of weight loss (because your mind is set that you cannot accomplish it). It is still doable, but you regard it as unachievable from a self-limiting perspective.

Think Different

Consider a charming tiny vintage wooden rowboat or a superyacht. Everything was just made out of wood, or the metaphor will collapse. Confidence is built into every panel of your boat's hull, which keeps you afloat as you sail the ocean. We must check that all of the sailing ship's boards are good and genuine — there must be no rotting wood or holes; otherwise, our boat would allow water to enter. What is this decaying plank symbolic for? It is a lack of trust that limits your commitment to your objective. It percolates and sows mistrust. It can even deflate your hopes if the situation is difficult enough.

Nathaniel Branden, the self-esteem expert, defines it as "the capacity to deal with life's essential obstacles and to be deserving of good fortune." Bear in mind that Branden did not state that you must be professional. You must have a positive self-image. And even if you are competent in a wide array of endeavors, you are not required to have experience. Choose one or two of them with which you are already familiar, and expand on them. Small steps.

The Mirror

When we delve deeper into your trust in your perceptions, we discover that your experiences (external occurrences) are led by your belief (internal events).
Then you can use extracurricular activities to ascertain your thoughts. It is frequently referred to as a mirror. You are living in a world that reflects your worldview. If you want to alter your experiences, you must alter your confidence.

Your lives are excellent teachers, but if you forget that you're in school, you risk failing the entire course. Indeed, it will be provided again, but you know what happens yearly! If you begin compiling a list of events, circumstances, or individuals that make you feel uneasy, they will come to mind as you work through the concepts in this book. These notes will serve as a starting point for future explorations of your mirror. Consider a person you are familiar with and explain how that individual could think and experience things. And how about you? Is there anything you'd instead not go through in your life? What do you think these encounters lead to?

How to remove limiting Beliefs

You can choose to eradicate limiting beliefs in the same way that you acquired them. Additionally, you can uninstall them using this option. That is your choice. It may sound oversimplified, but it works in this manner. Numerous validated strategies outline mechanisms for removing extra thinking, but the critical part of removal is selection. While the technical removal procedure is straightforward, it presents a mental hurdle for most people. Imagine walking on fire if you were told in a book that all you needed to do was focus on damp, humid, velvety grass. I doubt you'll take your shoes off until you've received some guidance. The techniques for disabling thought are identical. Before most people feel they can, confidence must be built on fewer instances of accomplishment. We are both sure of what is possible and what is not possible. To begin, they must be handled.

Additionally, it's a good idea to replace it with an inspiring one by overcoming a restrictive mindset. It is an eloquent illustration. Assume that the limiting belief "There's only something that needs to be worked out" has been revealed. To begin, focus your full attention on this belief, and then slowly and deliberately state to yourself, mentally or verbally, "I hold the conviction that nothing works for me, and I decide to remove it from my belief system, as it restricts me." (Perhaps you'd like to visualize the belief's energy dissipating or dissolving as you verbalize the release.) It consumes everything. Replace it with a new one. I want to replace it with, "all I do is in my best interest." It is the final tactic I've uncovered for individuals who believe in eradicating restricting beliefs—utilizing the technique of ignoring the flaws in your suspicions

Assume you wish to eliminate the limiting mindset. "No one listens to what I have to say." When you begin to say, "I'm not sure how I'm going to accomplish that properly." You are aware. That is the bare minimum level of confidence you are attempting to achieve. Begin with "I believe, and I want to eradicate the notion that I am incapable of performing this task properly since it limits me." Then you reflect, "I'm not sure it succeeded." "I have the conviction that 'I'm not sure that succeeded,' and I want to eliminate it because it constrains me." Then return to the original limiting belief: "Nobody cares what I have to say." When another issue arises before the initial restraining conviction is lifted, proceed in the same manner – eliminate it. Do not be surprised if any of these ugly doubts arise at first. Please pat yourself on the back and eliminate another. Continue.

Changing your beliefs

In this situation, if you want to change your success and results in any aspect of your life, you must shift your self-concept—or preconceptions about yourself. Convictions, fortunately, are always arbitrary. They are not always reliable sources of information. Rather than that, they are founded chiefly on facts, frequently with scant evidence you have taken in and accepted as reality. The worst beliefs are those that are self-limiting in some way. These are convictions that make you feel limited or defective in some way. Although this conviction is uncommon, you recognize it as an accurate assessment of your capacity and as correct for you as if it were real.

Challenge your self-limiting beliefs as a beginning point for unlocking your potential and achieving more than ever. You begin this process of liberation from self-limiting beliefs by supposing that they are wrong, regardless of what they are. Feel that your talents are infinite for the time being. Consider the possibility that you will be, do, or have anything in life that you enjoy Consider the possibility that your potential is limitless. Consider earning twice as much as you do today. Consider the possibility of living in a larger home, driving a better automobile, and enjoying a more economical way of life. Consider yourself to be a leader in your field. Consider yourself one of the most well-known, influential, and inspirational figures in your social and business circles. Consider yourself to be composed, trustworthy, and brave. Consider the possibility that you can direct your thoughts and achieve any goal. It is how you begin to improve your thinking and life.

The first step is to reprogram your mental hard drive with new, optimistic, constructive, and courageous thoughts about yourself and your future; this will eliminate your anxieties and allow your inner light to shine.

Three Pieces of Your Self Conception

Your creation of yourself is separated into three segments, similar to how a pie is divided into three wedges. Everyone is connected. All three elements encompass what you think, feel, and do and anything that happens to you.

Your self-ideal is the first component of your personality and self-conception. Your objectives, desires, visions, and ideas are within your self-ideal. Your self-ideal is composed of the traits, principles, and characteristics you and others most admire. These ideals guide and shape your activities. Their principles, aspirations, and beliefs exemplify outstanding men and women, leaders, and citizens of character. They have established lofty goals for themselves and are unwilling to abandon them. They are well aware of their identity and the values they espouse. They are men and women who others can go to for guidance and support. They are precise and distinct in their interactions with others. They endeavor to live up to their principles in all parts of their lives.

The second component of your self-concept is your self-image. It is how you see and think about yourself. Additionally, it is referred to as an "inner mirror." You look internally to determine how you will behave in a particular situation. Due to the power of your self-image, you continue to act on the outside, following your inner self-image. Maxwell Maltz's self-image development represents a significant advancement in human efficacy and performance. When you envision yourself succeeding in the following situation, you send a message to your subconscious mind. Your subconscious mind accepts this message and uses it to organize your thoughts, words, and actions following your vision. Any transformation in your life begins with a more positive mental image. Your interior images affect your emotions, behaviors, attitudes, and how others react to you. Developing a positive self-image is a necessary component of thought and behavior transformation.

The third component of your self-concept is your self-esteem. The emotional dimension of your personality significantly influences your cognition, feeling, and conduct. Your self-esteem dictates the majority of what occurs in your life. It is easiest to think about self-esteem in terms of how much you enjoy yourself. The more you desire, the more you will attempt anything. And, by the rule of reversibility, the more you do, the more you like yourself. Your self-esteem serves as the "reactor core" of your personality. It is your energy source that determines your level of trust and enthusiasm.

The more self-imposed standards you have, the more you like yourself. The more you desire, the loftier your ambitions become and the longer it takes to accomplish them. Individuals with a high sense of self-worth cannot hesitate. The more you adore and admire something, the more you desire and respect it, and the more content you are with it. The consistency of your interpersonal relationships is closely tied to your self-confidence. Your self-esteem will decide whether people will buy from you, hire you, work with you, or even give you money in your business and career; when you become a spouse and parent, your self-esteem increases. Parents with a high sense of self-worth produce children with a high sense of self-worth. These children are highly self-assured and develop strong bonds with other children who share high self-esteem. Through love, laughter, and happiness, self-esteem houses define people who live in them.

AFFIRMATION

Nothing is impossible; the very term declares, "I'm possible!"- **Audrey Hepburn.**

Words of affirmation are so pervasive, significant, and potent, yet so subtle, that we do not even recognize them as the underlying governor of our thoughts and life experiences. Words of affirmation have conditioned us in ways that most adults have not even considered. Affirmations are remarks we make to ourselves; they are our internal dialogue. Whether purposefully or unwittingly, you are constantly using affirmations. You have just formed a negative affirmation if, after making a mistake, you tell yourself, "I always make mistakes, and I never do anything correctly." You have just created a positive affirmation if, after committing an error, you tell yourself, "That's okay, I have the power to fix this." Your internal dialogue significantly impacts both your conscious and subconscious thoughts. By repeating positive affirmations, your mind patterns can be reprogrammed. Developing new thought patterns can enable you to alter your core beliefs and how you think and feel about yourself, others, and your role in the world. Through the use of daily positive affirmations, you can substantially enhance your life in this way.

Affirmation is a highly effective method for empowering one's subconscious. Once the subconscious is trained to accept an affirmation, it is transformed into positive action by the conscious mind. Individuals are encouraged to do, work, and strive for more through affirmation. Affirmation enables individuals to believe in themselves and act on their views. Affirmation combines vocal and visual techniques that mirror an individual's desired mental state. Strong affirmations can be highly effective, and virtually anyone can use them to attain his goals and satisfy his aspirations. However, the effectiveness of an affirmation depends on its strength or weakness.

Affirmation is essentially a person's declaration regarding something or a state of being. A person might affirm his desired outcomes, such as "I now have a happy life." The affirmation can also facilitate the attainment of mental, physical, and spiritual health. A powerful affirmation should be voiced in the present tense for greater effectiveness. An affirmation stating, "I am now a happy being" is more potent than one stating " I will become a happy being." Affirmations should always be positive because they are meant to work in your favor, not against you. Why not make the affirmation "I am joyful" instead of "I am not sad"? To be more effective, an affirmation should be composed of simple yet concise language and brief.

A lengthy affirmation might have the opposite effect of generating a positive outlook in a person. A person can readily speak and repeat a short affirmation. It can function as a mantra that can be repeated countless times. For an affirmation to be successful, it must be repeated. Repetition is effective and stimulates the subconscious, which pushes the individual to act on his affirmation. The creator of the affirmation must be emotionally invested in the words he will use to realize his affirmation. Creating an affirmation might benefit from the potency of writing words one believes in.

The parasite in our minds that keeps the past alive has prevented us from hardwiring our brains to experience a reflection of heaven with absolute tranquility and pure love. Every time we believe there are no problems, the past conditioning of the body and mind uncovers one. We can only live that way through the thoughts we choose to concentrate on now. To live like a lily, your thoughts must be as natural and transparent as the flower's growth. Regardless of the circumstances, we must accept life with an attitude of calm and wholeness. This action produces a future reaction of peace.
We must obtain command of our subconscious memory system and refocus our attention on numerous positive affirmations. We have been conditioned by school for most of our early years;

thus, you may need to unlearn some things. Whatever words of encouragement you plant in your mental garden will manifest in your physical world as objects and realities; now is the time to uproot and replant.

Affirmation for calming the mind

Have you ever found yourself mired in negative thought patterns, wishing your life looked different, wishing the people around you would change or believing that you are inadequate? Instead of searching outside for a new companion, new home, or higher accomplishments, you may get better results by altering your perception of your circumstances. Here, affirmations come into play. When speaking and thinking positively becomes a habit, the brain gradually rewires itself to generate positive rather than negative beliefs. If you frequently have negative ideas about yourself or your life, consider repeating one of the affirmations below. Repeat the affirmations every day and post them in a visible location (such as your bathroom mirror) for optimal effects.

- My yearning for peace is amply satisfied, as I am a funnel of peace and well-being.

- I embrace, love, and appreciate myself and who I am without conditions.

- I acknowledge and am grateful for the ongoing flow of abundance in my life.

- Because I exude serenity and love, I assist others in living in a condition of peace and love.

- I am an island of serenity, even surrounded by a sea of uncertainty.

- Presently, right here and now, everything is fine.

- I can overcome my past and live in peace and tranquility.

- I am aware of and appreciative of all the beauty surrounding me.

- I am capable of embracing love while releasing fear.

- The calming silence of my inner spirit brings me comfort.

- My mind is getting tranquil, allowing me to sleep soundly and healthily.

- My mind becomes free of unpleasant thoughts when I meditate.

- When I meditate, my mind is calm.

- In all conditions, I am calm, energized, and possessed of inner power.

- I can silence my mind and thoughts whenever I desire.

- I can calm my mind and body in any situation.

- Stress and anxiety have vanished, and calm and composure have taken their place.

- I have tranquil thoughts and peaceful existence.

MINDFULNESS

"You cannot stop the waves, but you can learn to surf," - **Jon Kabat-Zinn.**

Mindfulness is living in the moment, not living for the moment. When you are living for the moment, there are no potential consequences. You act in the now, doing something that makes you feel happy. But frequently, it is a shock to learn that costs are involved! When you are present, you are aware that one instant flows into the next and that life comprises a sequence of interconnected moments. You take responsibility for your decisions and make intentional decisions based on your views and ideals. At its most extreme, worrying about the future can lead to anxiety disorders.

According to research, the number of people who suffer from depression and anxiety has been rising gradually but consistently. 7.5% of people reported having anxiety and depression in 1993, but 9.7% reported these conditions in 2007. 4.45% of people in the population had a generalized anxiety disorder in 1993, which increased to 4.7 percent in 2007. When we feel overwhelmed by the past or the future, we are no longer in the present.

It's simple to lose track of what is happening in the one true instant by wasting "now" time. For instance, while working, you imagine yourself on vacation; while away, you worry about the work stacking up on your desk.

You can now bring your phone and computer on vacations and it makes things worse because you are never really anywhere! Computers and "smartphone" devices are just a few examples of how contemporary technology can cause you to become disconnected from the present and your surroundings. By being mindful, you can enjoy and live your life rather than hurrying through it while attempting to be somewhere else all the time. Being more mindful allows you to be in the present moment more frequently. It entails returning your focus to the current moment from the past or the future. You are already a better person and in the right place.

How frequently do you practice mindful living, accepting each moment of life as it comes without prejudging it? If you're like most people, you frequently attempt to juggle two or three tasks at once. And the majority of what you do probably happens automatically, without your awareness. For instance, let's say you decide to make yourself some tea. While waiting for the water to boil, you might start reading the paper, doing the dishes, or even making a phone call. Alternatively, you might start reflecting on a conversation you had the day before or planning your dinner for the evening.

You are not thinking about the tea or the current circumstance. It is easy to become so preoccupied with your thoughts and emotions about the past or future that you lose sight of what is occurring in the present. So, missing the full tea experience is not that big a deal! Of course, there are instances when focusing on more than two things at once enables you to do tasks swiftly and effectively.

The main challenges come when your mind wanders off to anxious thoughts about the past and the future, rehashing upsetting memories from the past and conjuring up the worst-case scenarios for the future. At their greatest extremes, being locked in the past or the future can result in sadness or anxiety.

There's nothing mystical about mindfulness. Being mindful is to pay attention to and participate in the present moment. It's all about living in the now. If you've ever lost yourself in a crossword puzzle, a board game, a song, a book, a movie, a letter you were composing, or work you were doing, then you've experienced mindfulness; you've been fully present. Watch a child playing; he isn't considering what happened yesterday or what he will do later

today. He's engrossed in whatever he's creating, pretending to be, or sketching; he screams and sobs when he is unhappy; nothing else matters to him but what has upset him. He will sob about it before letting it go and forgetting the offense.
Have you ever accompanied little children to the cinema?

Everything is fantastic and brand-new; they stare at the bright lights in the foyer. They are watching everyone seated nearby. They shake in their chairs as they admire the enormous screen and shudder when the music begins. When things get spooky, they leap onto your lap, and when things are humorous, they start laughing aloud. They live each moment.

You can become mindful at any moment. You can do it right now. Focus on what's happening around you; what can you hear? What are you smelling? Look straight ahead; what do you see? What can you feel? Don't think about it; you don't have to agree or disagree with what's happening or like or dislike it. You need to be aware of it.

Even if nothing is present, focus on your breathing instead. Feel the air entering your nose or mouth, filling your lungs, and then leaving your body again. Does all this seem a bit pointless?

How is this method of not acting of any use?

Let me explain.
The ability to think—to reflect on the past, consider the future, and make plans is a quality that distinguishes humans from other animals.

We can think about things besides just what is happening, such as:

- Things that did and didn't happen
- Things that have happened
- Things that might happen
- Things that may never happen at all.

Your mind is constantly thinking and dreaming. It's always busy, and you expect it just to keep going. Thoughts cannot be stopped, but they won't work properly if the mind isn't given a break.

By practicing mindfulness, you can vacation from your mind's constant chatter, similar to the commentary that comes with a sports program on television. Two things are going on at once: the game and the never-ending commentary. Turning off the sound allows you to play the game without having to play through someone else's thoughts. Your thoughts evaluate your experience and provide commentary on how difficult, wonderful, unfair, beautiful, incorrect, dull and everything else you may think it is.

Too frequently, it is possible to be swept away by a tidal surge of thoughts and emotions. Mindfulness and present-moment awareness offer a welcome respite from these taxing and repeated mental patterns.

Being mindful helps you stay grounded and in your center so that you are less affected by external events. You can better remain concentrated and maintain your composure through positive and negative situations. When your mind is overloaded and disorganized, it is challenging to "think straight" since it is difficult to see through the mental clutter. You can select between two courses of action more readily and clearly when mindful. This does not, however, imply that you adopt a strict way of thinking or acting. You can think more flexibly when you're mindful.

When you are conscious of how and what you are thinking, you can let go of long-standing patterns of behavior and be receptive to a novel, more beneficial ones. You will find that when you are mindful, you are less critical.

Being mindful helps you to experience things without passing judgment or doing any assessments or analyses. You can observe experience without getting sucked into it. You realize that whatever takes place is only tough, bad, wrong; if you think about it that way. In reality, mindfulness teaches you to recognize when your thoughts and self-talk have regressed into harmful patterns and the kinds of ideas and self-talk that feed your emotions. When attentive, you become more aware of the connections between your ideas, feelings, and behavior. You are less reactive and more responsive. What's the difference? Well, if you react, you're probably going to resist or disagree with what is happening. When you react, you act in a way that is suitable for the circumstance.

For instance, if you feel you have treated someone unfairly, your reaction can be to try and defend your actions or deny that you did anything wrong. When one is conscious, they are aware of their feelings and what they are trying to communicate. You are more inclined to make restitution for your errors in response to these regretful sentiments. Mindfulness can aid in the management of a variety of challenging emotions. You could use it, for instance, to reduce and manage anxiety and tension. When you concentrate on the present, what is occurring right now - worries and anxiety cannot enter your consciousness. Because you are more aware of the warning signs and can suppress the urge to respond instantly, mindfulness is a potent tool for controlling anger. You find that everything slows down in a way that makes it easier for you to react to challenging events in a much more composed manner. Your life becomes better in quality because you are better able to handle challenges and make the most of the positive things in it.

Being mindful enables you to immerse yourself in an activity and savor the moment fully. There are no thoughts about the "next" moment because you are so preoccupied with what is happening now; nothing can divert your attention.

Mindfulness liberates you from the obsession with your situation. Your eyes are opened to the world as it unfolds in front of you, including the sounds of birds, the shifting of the light, the flow of traffic, and everything else that is taking place right now. No matter how often birds have chirped, the light has changed, or the traffic has flown by, mindfulness can help you view things differently; you are open to new possibilities even in situations you are acquainted with.

Mindfulness turns a boring or routine activity into something new. It allows you to view things fresh and experience everything as if it were the first time. No matter how frequently you do anything, it will always be different; there will always be a different method. Thus, mindfulness enables you to let go of everything that restricts possibilities since it makes you open to new experiences. It gives you confidence and courage. You become more confident in yourself, more assured of your skills, and better able to carry out your good intentions and accomplish your objectives.

Aspects of mindfulness

- **Awareness.**

This entails paying attention to the ideas, experiences, and events taking place in the present moment while being conscious of them.

- **Acknowledgment.**

This is the recognition of the existence of something. Recognizing thoughts, feelings, experiences, and events as they happen is what mindfulness entails.

- **Acceptance.**

In this situation, nothing is being done; only the fact that events are occurring (or not) is being acknowledged. Knowing that thoughts, feelings, sensations, beliefs, and actions are merely thoughts, feelings, sensations, and beliefs is a necessary step toward acceptance. It's in the present moment that acceptance occurs.

- **Non-judgmental.**

This is merely experiencing or witnessing what is happening without evaluating it. To be non-judgmental, you must refrain from assigning any significance to your thoughts, feelings, or the behaviors or occurrences of others. You merely see things objectively rather than categorizing them as "excellent" or "bad." The only way that thoughts may have any significance is by relating them to experiences and events.

- **Letting go.**

This entails not clinging to or growing emotionally connected to thoughts, feelings, ideas, or experiences. Rather recognizing they are part of the past.

- **Focus and engagement.**

Focus, a distinct and defined point of attention or action, is necessary for mindfulness. It entails controlling your attention such that it is narrowly focused and engrossed with the present moment. You pay attention to one thing at a time.

- **Beginner's mind.**

The beginner's mentality can assist you in seeing things from a fresh perspective rather than reacting to situations in the same old, old-fashioned ways. You let go of your convictions and the decisions you made in the past, allowing yourself to be open to fresh possibilities in situations you are familiar with. You are aware of the minute adjustments that distinguish what is happening right now from what has happened in the past. Being aware of anything new brings you into the present moment because it makes you more conscious of the current situation.

- **Patience and trust.**

This aspect of mindfulness is knowing that everything happens in its own time.
It's critical to understand that these dynamic components and attributes of mindfulness— acceptance, awareness, beginner's mind and the other pieces. —are all crucial. Despite having unique qualities, each component is connected to and engages in interaction with others. So, for instance, if you approach a problem with a beginner's mind, you can probably let go of prior thoughts, ideas, ways of doing things. This implies that you may accept that past events are gone with the past.

Now that you know how and why practicing mindfulness can improve your life, it's time to start!

You'll see that practicing mindfulness only requires increasing your awareness of your thoughts. And there's more good news: you can develop more flexible, open thinking. Your mind is up for the challenge!

Mindfulness Meditations

For many, the mere notion of meditation and mindfulness evokes mental and physical stillness for extended periods. It is an image sufficient to turn many people away from these practices before they have even tried them. While skilled meditators frequently sit practically motionless for extended periods, it is counterproductive to any mindfulness practice to be preoccupied with a preconceived notion of how long one "should" meditate. Meditation and mindfulness's emotional and physical benefits include enhanced immunity, better heart health, less despair and anxiety, and sharper cognitive abilities.

According to Joshua Felver, professor of psychology at Syracuse University and director of the Mind Body Laboratory, one of the most incredible benefits of mindfulness is that it enhances every other element of your life by helping you improve decisions. "Regular mindfulness practice allows you to take a step back from stressors, allowing you to respond in an adaptive manner rather than in ultimately destructive ways." Felver explains, "mounting scientific evidence has demonstrated that mindfulness techniques lower the experience of stress and boost immune system functioning, providing a unique tool for enhancing one's body and mind even in tough conditions."

One of how mindfulness works is by helping to calm the autonomic, or "fight or flight," system, resulting in a cascade of calming brain chemicals. Since mindfulness is purely about moment-to-moment awareness, regardless of how long this awareness is maintained, the length of time we practice during any session is less important than simply turning up. In mindfulness practice, consistency is more important than duration. Beginning the journey into mindfulness by investigating short practices (or introducing extra micro mindfulness sessions into a well-established practice) is just as worthwhile as beginning with longer practices. Meditation can be used in a variety of ways to cultivate mindfulness. Simply put, it is aware of where your conscious attention is directed. What arises may be pleasant or disagreeable. However, as you practice this inside dive with non-judgmental attention, you can access this already-existing state of inner serenity. Anyone can begin a mindful meditation practice to achieve a new degree of tranquility. It's all about the discipline of sitting and introspection.

Practicing mindfulness Breathing

Once you have relaxed into your meditation posture, begin breathing through your nose and focus your attention on the simple feeling of breathing. Counting your breath might help to steady and stabilize your consciousness. This is accomplished by counting each breath and exhaling, beginning at one and proceeding to ten. After the inhalation, count one. Exhale and count two at the end of the exhale. Continue counting until you reach ten, then return to one and begin again. Maintain focus on your breath at all times, with the counting serving to keep you alert. When your mind begins to wander, and a concept develops that causes you to lose consciousness, you should perceive or notice the thought, then let it go and restart the count at one. In other words, anytime your attention wanders away from the breath to thought, or to a memory; you should become aware of this and return it to the breath. This helps you recognize when your mind has wandered. Each time you return your attention to your breath, you gain an essential part of mindfulness. This is of the utmost importance and is the foundation of all Buddhist meditation and practice.

During concentrating on the breath, the predominant thoughts, sensations, and emotions that arise will be simple, everyday things. At the same time, it is typical for things you let go of to return to your awareness after you release them. You repeatedly let something go, but it keeps coming back. This indicates that your process of letting go may take a little longer. Here, we underline the need to suppress neither nor become embroiled in one's thoughts and feelings. Shift your focus from the breath to the persistent object and allow it to exist in your awareness without engaging in a narrative. Because you are not holding to it, it should dissolve over time, and you can resume breathing awareness.

Dispersed mental activity and energy separate us from one another, our surroundings, and ourselves. As we begin to sit, the mental activity on the surface begins to slow down. When the wind blows, the mind resembles the surface of a pond; the surface is disturbed, ripples form, and silt from the bottom is moved. Although the water is naturally clear and pristine, it is impossible to see beneath the surface. Yet, amid this innate quiet, our life's boundless vitality emerges. If we do not understand it clearly, we may never have the chance to reach a place of peace. The deeper your body rests, the more thoroughly your mind is at peace. The body reaches a level of quiet that is not reached even during deep sleep. This is an essential and natural component of being human. It is not an exceptionally uncommon occurrence. The capacity to be awake is a crucial component of being alive!

Additionally, it is essential to be patient and steady. Try to let go of whatever expectations and objectives you may have for yourself. No matter your religious views, meditation is a practice to open a new way to view ourselves and our existence, even though we're conditioned to function in this way in everyday life. Devote yourself to zazen and let go of your thoughts, opinions, and stories. There are many forms of meditation, zazen is one form of sitting meditation. The human mind is unfettered, expansive, alive, and calm. Zazen teaches us to uncover the mind, see who we are, and experience the world as it truly is.

Gratitude Meditation

There will be occasions when you become emotionally invested in the things and circumstances you desire, making it challenging to be in the present. However, it is impossible to stay mindful if you are obsessed with the past or the future. Concentrating on what you didn't get and what you believe you need is tempting rather than enjoying what you currently have.

As the Tibetan saying goes, "the moment we are content, we have enough."

The issue is that we approach things from the wrong direction, believing that we won't be happy until we have enough. Perhaps you wish to relocate to a bigger home or a better neighborhood because you don't like where you now reside. Maybe you're upset that you didn't receive the desired job or that your friend had a better holiday season than you. What can release you from your attachment to past failures or future wants? Gratitude comes naturally when you take note of the little pleasures around you, no matter how small and trivial they may seem. Gratitude is strongly and persistently connected with an increased sense of satisfaction and well-being. According to science, counting blessings boosts our optimism, alleviates depression, boosts immune function, and decreases blood pressure. Additionally, it deepens our interactions with others in our immediate vicinity. Gratitude meditation is the simple process of reflecting on the aspects of our lives for which we are grateful. It's about experiencing that sense of gratitude, whether it's for a devoted family member or friend, a lovely sunny day, or the enjoyment of a nice cup of coffee.

Have you ever considered the circumstances that have transpired in your life? Allow sufficient time to reflect on your life and experiences. It's time to act after identifying your attitude, legacy, and self-empowerment cost. It's time to conduct a reflexive self-assessment by assessing your life, reflecting on, evaluating, and paying close attention to your behaviors, attitudes, cost, and legacy. Consider the good, the bad, and the ugly elements of it. Consider both the happy and unpleasant occurrences in your life. That is the primary lesson.

Consider the information you've gathered. Life is wondrous!

The majority of people are perpetually on the move. As a result, people hardly ever pause to consider their life. Would you mind taking time to reflect on your life and how you live it? If you don't do it deliberately, you'll be trapped in a cycle with no way out. Evaluate your performance following each occasion, day, week, month, and year.

Life serves as a teacher, imparting vital wisdom to us. When it teaches you something, create the habit of constructively applying what you've learned, and you'll be more equipped to use your understanding to empower and enhance the lives of others. What accomplishments did you make yesterday, and how will you improve today? Life is a decision, not a byproduct of chance. Individuals who prosper in life intentionally cultivate their luck element.

Experience is costly; it enables you to assess your capabilities before going on an adventure. It is more costly not to analyze and learn from it, as it is infuriating to pay for experience but not receive the lesson, as is frequently the case with some people. Every interaction should teach something valuable and positive, not merely something to pass the time.

The school of life offers a variety of courses. We choose to be a part of some of them, while others find us unintentionally. Everyone has valuable things to teach us, but only if we are willing to learn and reflect on them. If you can maintain your composure when everyone is blaming you, if you can believe in yourself when everyone else doubts you, if you are willing to pay the price and go the extra mile for success, the world and everything associated with you is yours. You must recognize your potential and take control of your life. Maintain awareness of your higher life, re-dedicate yourself, and seize control. While you're doing it, remember to express gratitude for your own and others' lives.

Gratitude for your life can be the difference between having an enriched, joyful, and contented life and living an unenriched, unhappy life. When you show thankfulness, even the little details of your life get magnified and appreciated. You begin to derive pleasure from every moment and episode in your life. In this state of thankfulness, your energy is increased, and you feel fulfilled.

Start with something small.

If you're not sure what to be grateful for, start small. At a minimum, begin with something you take for granted daily. Express gratitude for a warm, comfy bed in which you may snuggle each night while resting in bed. What about your cozy blanket? And while you're lying there, let your mind stray to other people who are without a bed or a blanket and offer them love and comfort. Pray for them, and your thankfulness will soar to new heights. It may be an enlightening exercise, even more so if we're whining about how awful our lives are. Take it a step further and assist someone in need.

Exhibit gratitude

While your partner, children, and friends are still around, this is an appropriate time to show your gratitude. Do not wait until your children reach adulthood to express gratitude for their presence in your life; if you had never expressed gratitude for their presence when they were still living at home, now is an opportune moment to begin.

Express your gratitude to your lover; this could be the moment that draws you two closer together. When others assist you or do something nice for you, you can express your gratitude and appreciation in various ways. It is critical because people respond to recognition, and if you do not demonstrate your appreciation for them, the likelihood of them doing something else for you is small. When you expect what someone will do for you, expressing gratitude entails delivering the other person's positive strokes, sadly lacking in many spheres of life.

With a smile, express your gratitude.

One of the most critical components of expressing thankfulness is your words and how you say them. Simply mentioning those two phrases demonstrates your gratitude for their assistance. The grin is critical because it matches your words, indicates your friendliness, and heightens the other person's sense of gratitude. When you exit a bus or an airplane or work as a food server in a restaurant, you can brighten someone's day by simply saying "thank you."

Make gratitude a mindset and a lifestyle.

When gratitude becomes a habit, you will approach everything with a grateful attitude. Practice gratitude from the minute you wake up in the morning, throughout the day, and just before you sleep. A grateful heart radiates joy and connects you to tranquility. When life throws a curveball at you, search for the silver lining, even if it's the tiniest, and change into thanksgiving mode. You'll develop an appreciation for everything and refuse to take anything for granted. Once the first excitement wears, familiarity compels us to take things for granted. On the other hand, gratitude renews our appreciation each day and enables us to see the familiar in new ways. Now that you've found your shortcomings through this checkbook, you're free from the chains of life and in control of the areas of your life where you've been unable to improve yourself.

Healing Depression with Mindfulness

Mindfulness is the art of listening to our inner feelings and caring for those painful emotions that lie at the core of depression, anxiety, fear, and other forms of persistent emotional stress that undermine our happiness and adversely affect our relationships. However, this quality of mindful listening, of knowing with mindfulness, is not the same as thinking about our suffering or trying to understand why we are unhappy. Analytical thinking can be a helpful strategy and forms a part of the therapeutic healing process. Still, understanding is seldom enough to resolve the inner pain of depression or anxiety. We have to shift to a much more subtle level of experience, below the level of the thinking mind: the realm of feeling itself.

An emotion like depression is formed when feeling energy becomes trapped within the mental structures of thoughts and beliefs. It is not the thoughts or beliefs that are the problem, but the emotional feeling energy invested in the thought or belief. If we can learn to release this trapped energy, the thought/belief becomes harmless, stripped of its power, and much easier to change. We know we must let go of negative thoughts such as "I am a useless person. I can't cope. I feel unloved." The difficulty is in how to let go because the emotions are so strong that they overwhelm and enslave us, and we habitually become them over and over again. Effective letting go is not an activity of the thinking mind and not an act of willpower, but something that happens naturally as we begin to dissolve the emotional part of the thought objects that keep us bound. This compulsive-obsessive energy is the real problem, and there can be no letting go until it is resolved.

Mindfulness begins when we can look at an emotion thought memory-belief as an object, a mental object that we can observe and investigate, in the same way, that a scientist might investigate a new life form. This is quite different from our usual blind reactivity of becoming the emotion and wallowing in the patterns of harmful and destructive thinking. When we establish mindfulness, we let go of thinking about the emotion and direct our attention to the feeling quality, the felt sense of anxiety, depression, sorrow, or grief. We focus on the feeling energy of the mental object rather than the contents or story. This energy is often associated with sensory feelings such as blackness, heaviness, and dullness and is frequently felt in the stomach, heart, or other parts of the body. Mindfulness is the conscious awareness and investigation of this feeling energy.

Now, this is when it gets interesting. When we learn to sit mindfully with this energetic quality of our mental objects, the emotions, thoughts, memories, perceptions, and beliefs that make up our experience, the whole scene changes. The emotions become malleable and pliable and regain the plasticity lost when we become reactive and blindly follow habitual emotional reactions. Emotional plasticity is an essential concept in mindfulness psychology and central to healing.

Reactivity inhibits plasticity and creates rigidity, which results in mental suffering. Mindfulness reverses this process and restores emotional plasticity, and promotes the transformation and resolution of anxiety, depression, and other forms of suffering caused when feeling energy becomes frozen around mental constructs. There is growing evidence that mindfulness based emotional plasticity is closely associated with brain plasticity. As we practice the mindfulness response to our inner emotional distress, the brain circuits that determine how we perceive and respond to our suffering are altered.

Mindfulness has a direct healing effect, like sunlight's warming effect that promotes healthy growth. When you shine mindfulness on any part of the mind in pain, that mindfulness heals and resolves the pain, it can be likened to the sun shining onto a block of ice (our inner emotional pain); the ice melts by itself, without any struggle or effort required other than keeping the sunlight shining onto the ice. It is the same way with mindfulness. We create a healing space around the suffering when we focus mindfulness on the felt sense of our grief, anxiety, or suffering. Let go of the contents and focus on sitting with the feelings. Be fully present with the feelings, not trying to fix or struggle with them, but be fully present with them, knowing them as they are and taking the time to listen in silence. You will be surprised at what unfolds and the natural healing that occurs when you respond to suffering with mindfulness.

Sit down, close your eyes, choose to sit with your pain. Please don't indulge in thinking about the emotion; feel it and stay mindful of the feeling. This means also being vigilant of any tendency to react to the feelings or become seduced by the content of the emotion. When it happens, return your attention to the feeling and re-focus your mindfulness on the feeling. Stay present with compassion and an open heart and watch, listen and know what unfolds. This active presence, the essence of mindfulness, heals as sure as the gentle warmth of the sun gives new life the chance to spring forth from the dark, cold earth.

Intuition and Meditation.

We can all recall a moment (or countless cases) when our "gut" advised us not to begin a new relationship, accept a particular job, or even take an alternative route to work. Still, we ignored it and were likely to regret it later. Intuition is the inherent wisdom bestowed to us by the creator, and it can become a great resource if we develop a habit of listening to and believing it. This technique requires some time spent in silence and seclusion. Often referred to as "gut feelings," Intuition emerges holistically and rapidly, without awareness of the brain's underlying information processing. Scientists have repeatedly demonstrated that information can register in the brain without conscious awareness and positively affect decision-making and other behaviors. Intuition is a repository for your instincts, perceptions, and life experiences. We have our personal experiences, the experiences we have witnessed, and the emotional and cognitive processes we have developed over time. It is an emotional issue, not a matter of logic or reason. It is the capacity to perceive something approaching before its occurrence, even if there is no rational explanation. Your senses are all activated. After shaking someone's hand during an event, you could experience discomfort. You may have intense emotions due to your intuitive sense of something wrong. Most frequently, emotional Intuition is expressed through the heart.

Listening to our hearts is not the same as allowing our emotions, feelings, and desires to drive our opinions and behavior.

The intuitive understanding of the heart lies behind everyday feelings and emotions. Heart-based counsel and insights that might aid us in navigating life's daily ups and downs are invaluable, and we seldom regret listening to and trusting our hearts.

Becoming aware of your daily emotions and experiences is an excellent method to cultivate and improve heart centered intuitive awareness. Although our emotional energy is complicated, we are most conscious of our current and recent emotions and the emotions we aspire to experience. Typically, we are aware of our feelings toward the people we interact with frequently and the emotions we generate in our current state. Our emotions facilitate the formation of our likes and dislikes, preferences, and decision-making. We continually undergo new experiences. Our emotions are essential to our well-being and inherent to who we are. Therefore, we cannot exist without them. Even when we are confused or ignorant of our feelings, emotional energy circulates and moves through us. When confronted with negative emotions such as rage, fear, or grief, we often conceal and dismiss them.

Nonetheless, they continue to affect our lives and stay a part of us. Awareness of our daily emotions and feelings improves self-awareness and well-being. A more profound connection with and appreciation for the complete gamut of our emotions can also help us identify and comprehend our intuitive feeling.

How to Trust Your Intuition

It is critical to develop an ability to trust your Intuition. We all have intuitive thoughts, but we rarely acknowledge them. The most effective technique to develop trust in your Intuition is to engage in intuitive analysis. It's a relatively straightforward procedure. When confronted with a choice, consider the optimal course of action. You will receive many responses and alternatives, but one of these options will feel more "right" than the others. Numerous possibilities may be perfectly sensible and logical, but this one thing, this one decision, will feel entirely correct in your heart. This is the alternative suggested by your Intuition, and it is 99 percent of the time the best course of action. The objective is to acknowledge that the option that "feels right" is the one you must take; it is an emotion, a sensation, or a more profound understanding with any logical or reasonable foundation. If you pick this intuitive path and it proves optimal, your confidence in your Intuition will grow. Then all that remains is gradually increasing your confidence in your intuitive reasoning. This is the process by which confidence is established. There is no other way.

Intuition is a critical life talent that everyone must develop and refine, preferably sooner rather than later. Without Intuition, we become trapped in mazes of little, angry, or obsessive ideas that impair our ability to perceive clearly. The less clearly we perceive, the more likely we will make poor choices. When we follow our Intuition, we gain a sense of clarity that enables us to make the best choices for our lives.

We can develop our ability to trust our Intuition in a variety of ways:

- **Quiet your mind**

  Our minds frequently hijack our decision making processes. While it is critical to reason, your everyday thinking is frequently influenced by prejudice, prior beliefs, external pressures ("peer pressure"), and fear. To access your Intuition, you must empty your mind of all thoughts. I propose you meditate, listen to relaxing music, or focus on mindful breathing techniques to clear your mind.

  When you're worried, it's tough to listen to your instincts! For example, you could try deep breathing for a few minutes. Allow your tummy and chest to expand as you slowly breathe in through your nose. Then, to the count of four, take a deep breath in for four seconds, hold it for four seconds, and then exhale gently for four seconds. Any technique that soothes and stills your mind should be tried. You can accurately access your intuitive strength only when you are calm and balanced.

- **Consider the question: "How do I feel about this decision?"**
After you've calmed your mind and body, ask yourself, "How do I feel about this decision/situation/person?" inside. Take note of the first emotion, sensation, word, or image that comes to mind. Could you not give it too much thought? Remember that your initial impression is typically the most accurate, so stick with it. You should note down any ideas that spring to mind and consider them further.

- **Pay attention to your body's sensations.** Our bodies are like ultra-reliable truth detectors, alerting us to the range of pleasure, pain, and everything in between. Connecting with your body is a robust approach to learning to trust your

Intuition. Our bodies will always tell the truth, no matter how sophisticated the stories or hypotheses our minds concoct! To connect with your Intuition, think about anything weighing on your mind, such as a big decision, and pay attention to your body's reaction. For example, if you wish to quit your work, you might feel a wave of relief sweep over your entire body (which indicates that you should quit!). Alternatively, if you're considering moving to a new town, you might notice that your shoulders and neck stiffen up (which is most likely an indication that you shouldn't!). You can connect more freely with your Intuition if you practice body-centered mindfulness.

- **Examine whether you're being propelled by fear.**
Fear has a cunning way of passing for Intuition. Because of how powerful the mental voice inside us may become when we're afraid, we tend to make reckless decisions or assume we're
"following our instincts." Try putting down all of your anxieties about a circumstance on a piece of paper when you're faced with a big decision. This easy action will assist you in

creating more significant inner space and clarity and increase your trust in your Intuition. You'll be able to tell if the voice within you is fueled by fear or clear, intuitive awareness if you make your worries visible.

- **Come up with a conclusion and put both scenarios into practice.**
Another technique to improve your Intuition is brainstorming various solutions to the problem and mentally playing out each scenario. Consider each possibility as clearly as possible, then pay attention to how it feels in your heart and body. The one that feels the most "right" is the one you should choose. For example, if you're trying to decide whether or not to have an awkward talk with someone, you might consider the following options:

- Discuss over supper.
- Postpone the discussion until the following week.
- Initiate the conversation in a lighthearted manner.
- Postpone the talk until it's required. Then you'd imagine each scenario and notice how it made you feel. Whichever road you feel intuitively pulled to (even if your

head doesn't agree with it) is the one to follow.

- **Don't be swayed by peer pressure.** Do you place undue pressure on yourself? The need to make a "quick decision" hinders intuitive thought. While Intuition can be helpful in stressful situations, if you have the opportunity to calm down, please do so. Just because you aren't consciously worrying about something doesn't mean it isn't rising in your subconscious mind. Putting decisions on the back burner might help you relax, embrace new viewpoints, and open up to the presence of your intuitive knowledge more efficiently. As a result, sometimes, you need to take a step back to trust your instincts and know that you're on the right track.

- **Increase your self-awareness**

Self-awareness is the capacity to identify and understand your emotions, thoughts, and behaviors, as well as how they affect you and others. The more observant we are of ourselves, the easier it will be to notice our Intuition's soft voice in the first place. Self-awareness can be developed through mindfulness, meditation, and introspection. Start writing as a straightforward approach to start trusting your Intuition.

Ways to practice Mindfulness.

While mindfulness may sound like a good notion, how do you practice mindfulness throughout a hectic workday? You may be juggling emails, phone calls, meetings, and presentations. Naturally, your creation!
How can you employ mindfulness techniques to feel more alive and present while remaining productive?

Here are a few popular and radical methods for practicing mindfulness at work.

1. Be Consciously Present

Above all, mindfulness is about being aware and alert rather than operating unconsciously. When you are consciously present at work, you are aware of two dimensions of your moment-to-moment experience: what is happening around you and within you. Being aware at work entails being fully present in your work, both while and after it is completed, and controlling your mental and emotional condition. For example, if you're writing a report, mindfulness requires that you give it your undivided attention. When your mind wanders to Helen's new position or Michael's disagreement with the boss, notice the ideas and refocus on the task (see how to stop thinking). While this scenario appears straightforward, numerous facets of your experience can complicate matters.

At the beginning of each workday, make a deliberate decision to be as present as possible. Before beginning your workday, take a few moments to create this objective mentally.

2. Incorporate brief mindful exercises into your workday

Aware exercises help your brain develop a more mindful state of mind. The more mindful activities you perform, the easier it is for your brain to enter a mindful state, boosting brain function. Finding time for a 30-minute mindful workout might be challenging in a hectic office. Thus, does this imply that you cannot be conscious at work? Nope. The duration of mindful exercises is entirely up to you. Even one minute spent connecting intentionally with one of your senses qualifies as a mindful workout. You are not required to shut your eyes. You are not even required to be seated. Consider how you can carve out time during the day to practice mindfulness exercises. A brief mindfulness exercise can be a lifesaver when confronted with extreme work pressure. The procedure assists in rebalancing your neurological system by suppressing the fight-or-flight reaction and activating the intelligent part of your brain, allowing you to make rational judgments rather than reacting automatically to situations.

3. Be a lone wolf

Single-tasking is the act of concentrating on a single task at a time. Multitasking is attempting to complete two or more things concurrently or switching back and forth between tasks. Nobody is truly capable of multitasking. Your brain constantly switches between tasks, frequently losing information in the process. Nowadays, the majority of individuals understand that multitasking is useless. Why do people continue to multitask if it is so inefficient? Zheng Wang of Ohio State University discovered the explanation in a study. She observed students and discovered that they felt more productive when multitasking, even though they were inefficient. According to other research, the more you multitask, the more addicted you become to it.

Here is a tip for eliminating the multitasking habit and becoming a mindful superhero:

- Keep a time log of what you accomplish throughout a given time. Determine when you are performing a single task and when you are performing a multitasking task. Note what you accomplished within that period and how alert you were.

4. Utilize Conscious Reminders

The term "mindful" refers to the ability to recall. Most people who have read about or participated in mindfulness training understand the benefits of mindful living. Regrettably, people continue to forget to be careful! You lose track of mindfulness because your brain's natural (default) behavior is to become lost in your thoughts—to run a type of internal narrative. While performing routine daily tasks, your brain changes you into this low-energy state that is unmindful, almost dreamlike. While performing specific tasks mechanically, without thinking, is acceptable, Harvard University research indicates that up to 47% of a person's day can be lost in contemplation. The same study discovered that daydreaming could have a detrimental effect on one's wellbeing. Being on autopilot means you are not fully present and aware of the opportunities and choices you offer yourself. You cannot be creative, plan anything fresh, or respond effectively if you are acting mechanically.

By employing some reminders, you can reclaim your mindfulness. The reminder jolts you awake from the autopilot. Consider Using a phone alarm, a vibrating sound that does not disturb others can be compelling. As a result, whenever your phone calls, take a sharp breath. Each time you hear a text message ping, you take a moment to be conscious of your surroundings rather than quickly scanning the message. These are opportunities to re-enter the present moment and see yourself and your environment from a new perspective. You take a tiny step back and contemplate rather than automatically react to your demands, tasks, and obstacles.

5. Slow Down To Speed Up

At first glance, mindfulness at work appears counter-intuitive. You're considering how you can improve your efficiency, productivity, happiness, resilience, and overall health at work by pausing or slowing down. You may be skeptical that slowing down and becoming more aware can have such an effect.

Consider being asked to forego sleep for a week. Sleep is a form of rest—and rest is not working. Therefore, refrain from resting and continue working. Perhaps you've encountered this when studying for exams or attempting to fulfill a work deadline. Eventually, your efficiency plummets to near nothing; you are utterly disconnected from the current moment and may even have hallucinations! To function successfully, you must sleep at least seven hours per night. Rest, without a doubt, can improve efficiency. If you can obtain approximately seven hours of sleep and accomplish a particular amount of work, consider what might happen if you added a few mini-mindfulness exercises to your day. Your brain would become even more efficient, concentrated, and successful at communicating with others.

Being in a panicked rush results in poor judgment and is a waste of energy. Rather than that, halt, concentrate on listening, hike rather than run, and take your time at work in general. Influential leaders, employees, and entrepreneurs take time to pause and deliberate to make the most significant judgments and actions possible—they slow down to accelerate. That is a conscientious approach to work.

6. Learn to embrace stress

Recent research from the University of Wisconsin Madison asked the same question of 30,000 people:
"Does the notion that stress affects health matter?" The outcomes were astounding.
The researchers discovered that those under a lot of stress but believed that stress was beneficial had among the lowest mortality rates. Highly stressed individuals believed stress was detrimental to their health and had the highest risk of death. Your ideas about stress have a significant impact on how they affect your health and wellbeing. Another study discovered that persons who believed stress was harmful tightened their blood vessels (as seen in patients with heart disease) but remained open and healthy when they believed stress was beneficial. If reading this did not make you say "wow," reread. It is the most intriguing piece of study I've read this year! Therefore, if you want to stress your friend, you must alter your perspective on it and, consequently, your body's response.

Mindfulness can assist you in bringing about this shift in perception. When you face a problem at work, pay attention to how your heart and breathing rates increase. Observe these behaviors and then alter your attitude—respond creatively rather than adversely to your stress. Be appreciative of the stimulating effect of the stress response. Take note that your body is preparing you for the forthcoming battle by increasing your heart rate, which circulates more oxygen throughout your body. Be appreciative of the process's ability to sharpen your senses and strengthen your immune system. By approaching the stress reaction in this manner, you might view your impending difficulty as a positive challenge and identify your body preparing to meet it. This minor adjustment to your mindset can practically add years to your life and boost your productivity and accomplishments at work.

7. Feel Gratitude

Humans suffer from a "negativity bias." It indicates that you are far more prone to fixate on something wrong than on something that has gone right. Daily behavior results in adopting an excessively negative and imbalanced thinking style.

Gratitude serves as an antidote. Numerous studies indicate that actively practicing thankfulness improves one's mood and benefits creativity, health, working relationships, and work quality. Gratitude enhances both job and home life. If you're trapped in a job you despise, the first step is to practice gratitude. How is your employment going? Perhaps you're appreciative of the money? Even if it is less than you desire, it is likely preferable to having no wage at all. You may dislike your manager, but are you pals with a few of your coworkers? You despise office politics, but they teach you what you don't like in a job, so you'll know what to seek in the future. After practicing thankfulness, you can decide whether to stay in that role or seek employment elsewhere.

Awareness of what is going well at work aids in developing resilience. Rather than allowing your mind to spiral into anxiety or bad moods as you stew over all the things about your job that you dislike, you can feed your mind with grateful ideas to boost your wellbeing. Then, if you decide to look for another employment, your good mental state can assist you in selecting a good position and optimize your interview performance. People hire optimistic individuals, not those who constantly moan about what is wrong. Utilize thankfulness to offset your brain's inherent negativity bias.

8. Develop an Attitude of Humility

Humble people possess quiet confidence in themselves and are unconcerned with constantly reminding others of their accomplishments. Humility may appear at odds with our culture's tendency to glorify individuals who make the most noise about themselves and capture our attention. However, humility is attractive—no one appreciates being around those who constantly sing their praises. Most people prefer to be around those prepared to listen to them rather than constantly talking about themselves.

In his enormously successful book Good to Great, Jim Collin selected CEOs who transformed good firms into exceptional ones. He discovered that the organizations with the most significant long-term success (at least 15 years of outstanding development) had leaders who possessed all of the characteristics of a typical leader but added one— personal humility. They were prepared to work diligently, not for themselves—or the corporation. If something went wrong, they did not seek to defend themselves by blaming others. And if things went well, they instantly looked to others to express gratitude. They did not have an inflated ego that required constant protection.

While humility is frequently confused with meekness or timidity, the two are not synonymous. Humility does not imply inferiority; rather, it implies an awareness of your inherent dependence on and equity with others around you. How are humility and mindfulness related? Accepting yourself as you are and being receptive to listening to and learning from others is what mindfulness is all about. Additionally, mindfulness is linked with gratitude— you recognize how others have aided you. And someone appreciative of others' contributions is inherently humble.

Mindfulness reduces activity in the portion of the brain that develops your self-story — sometimes referred to as the narrative self. It is harmful to devote excessive time to yourself and your tale. Mindfulness practice enables you to develop a stronger connection between your senses to your present self. Your perspective broadens, and you become aware of how others contribute to your daily triumphs.

9. Accept What You Are Powerless To Change

Acceptance is essential to mindfulness. Being aware entails accepting the current moment precisely as it is. And it means accepting yourself exactly as you are. It does not imply resignation or surrender. However, it does require accepting the reality of how things are at the moment before attempting to change anything.

Consider the following workplace scenario. If you exceeded your budget by $30,000, it is a fact. It has already occurred. Once you accept this, you can proceed and attempt to resolve the matter. Lack of acceptance might result in denial (which may cause you to go even farther over budget), avoidance (you continue to miss meetings with your boss), or violence (you vent your anger at your team unnecessarily, adversely affecting relationships and motivation). Rather than that, you can accept the situation, speak with the appropriate individuals, learn from your mistakes, and move on. Acceptance, on the other hand, results in a change.

Accepting yourself reduces energy-sucking self-criticism. You'll then be more capable of appreciating your accomplishments and laughing at your failures.

Acceptance on a personal level is even more potent. Acceptance entails embracing all elements of oneself—weaknesses, failings, aspects one dislikes and admires. Accepting yourself reduces energysucking self-criticism. You'll then be more capable of appreciating your accomplishments and laughing at your failures. Self-acceptance enables you to achieve a state of mind that enables you to work on the qualities you wish to change. Self-acceptance is the starting step for self-improvement and personal development.

10. Adopt a Growth Mindset

According to Carol Dweck at Stanford University, people have one of two mindsets: a development mindset or a fixed mindset. People with a fixed mindset thought that their fundamental characteristics, such as intelligence and abilities, are fixed. Rather than cultivating their knowledge and abilities, they spend their time hoping their characteristics will result in success. They do not seek personal development because they believe that talent alone guarantees success. They are proven to be incorrect—brain research has established the contrary.

Individuals with a growth mindset believe that they may increase their intelligence and talents with enough effort. They believe that by devoting themselves, they may improve. They view intelligence and talent as a starting point and build on them through diligence and commitment. Brain scans have indicated that working overtime increases intelligence and enhances initial talent. Individuals with this attitude value education and exhibit more resilience. Success in work requires a progressive mentality.

Adopting a growth mentality is key to mindfulness. Rather than analyzing your inherent talent or intelligence, mindfulness is about paying attention to the present moment and keeping open to new chances. When you have a growth mentality at work, you are unfazed by negative feedback because you view it as an opportunity to improve. You're not opposed to taking on additional tasks because you're intrigued about how you'll handle them.

You anticipate and embrace difficulties, viewing them as chances for inner growth. That is the essence of workplace mindfulness:

- Trusting in your ability to improve and grow through experience.

- Conquering challenges.

- Living in the moment.

- Learning new things about yourself and others.

4 Steps for Adopting a Growth Mindset

Follow the four steps mentioned below, which are based on Dweck's research, to develop a growth mindset:

1. In your thinking, listen to the voice of a fixed mindset. It is about being aware of one's ideas when confronted with a problem. Consider whether your thoughts are telling you that you lack talent or intelligence or whether you react with fear or anger when someone provides you critique.

2. Take note of the fact that you have a choice. You can either embrace or challenge those fixed mindset beliefs. Consider practicing a thoughtful pause for a few moments.

3. Put your fixed thinking attitudes to the test. When your ingrained attitude asks, "What if I fail?" You may ask yourself, "I'll be a failure," or "Is that true?" The majority of successful people fail. That is how kids acquire knowledge." Or if fixed thinking declares, "What if I am unable to complete this project?" I lack the necessary skills," respond with "Can I be certain I lack the necessary skills?" In reality, I will only know if I attempt. And if I lack the necessary skills, this will assist me in acquiring them."

4. Take action in the direction of a growth mentality. It can help you appreciate workplace challenges, viewing them as improvement opportunities rather than obstacles to overcome. Utilize the preceding approach whenever your mind begins to go toward fixed thinking. Over time, you'll develop a growth mindset rather than a fixed

attitude, resulting in more extraordinary achievement and personal mastery.

CONFIDENCE IS AN ABILITY

"By realizing one's potential and having faith in one's talents, one can contribute to the creation of a better world." - **Dalai Lama.**

While some people are born confident and brave, learning to speak up for their ideas and sell their expertise does not come easy to introverts. Thus, does this suggest that you are born with confidence, and others who are significantly less gifted in this area must muddle through as best they can? Confidence is not a set of standards that can be learned; confidence is a state of mind. Positivity, method, training, knowledge, and conversing with others are realistic ways to raise or improve your confidence. Confidence is generated by physical sensations, acceptance of one's mind and body (self-worth), and belief in ability, skills, and experience. Self-confidence is a characteristic that the vast majority of individuals wish they possessed.

Therefore, what exercises do the experts suggest for individuals who lack self-assurance and wish to learn how to retain their calmness in front of others? Initially, you should disregard reducing your stress and worry, heightening your self-consciousness.

Then consider honing and conforming to these abilities:

▪ Knowing your body signals

You can create a confidence issue by going above and beyond your own unique usual enhanced readiness. However, if you can work yourself up simply by misinterpreting your body's signals, you can work yourself down by reading them correctly. The irony is that misreading your nervous system's signals can help you perform better. Increased activation does not indicate failure but that you wish to succeed and your body is preparing to assist you."

▪ Focus on helping others

"Acquiring social capacities necessitates a change in one's self-esteem. Rather than being

137

uncomfortable and focusing exclusively on your anxiety, focus on building satisfying relationships that make those around you feel involved and joyful.

Concentrating less on oneself and more on others will result in significant benefits in terms of expanded social chances." Additionally, "having a genuine sense of commitment to a more significant cause can make your agony more acceptable."

- **Planning and Preparation**

Individuals are frequently pessimistic when confronted with novel or potentially tricky conditions. Probably the most critical component of developing confidence in planning and preparation for the unknown. For example, if you're interviewing for a new position, it's undoubtedly a good idea to prepare for the interview. Prepare what you wish to say and consider several of the questions you may be asked. Practice your responses with trustworthy friends or colleagues and education, training, and knowledge.

Discovering and conducting research can make us feel even more confident about our capacity to manage circumstances, functions, and activities. Understanding what to expect and how and why things are performed will heighten your awareness, make you feel more prepared, and make you more specific. There are multiple further examples of meeting planning. How will you get to the interview, and how long will the journey take? What clothing should you wear? Take control of strange events to the extent possible by breaking jobs into smaller sub-tasks and strategizing as much as possible.

It may be vital to have backup plans in case your primary plan fails under certain circumstances.

How would you ensure arrival if you meant to get to your interview by car, but the engine failed to start in the morning? Confidence is demonstrated by one's ability to respond comfortably to the unexpected.

- **Abundance mindset.**

A worldview of abundance entails seeing life's boundless potential. This implies that you can recognize the potential in both yourself and those around you. As a result, you actively work toward building the life you desire. An abundance mindset is predicated on the assumption that there is a limitless supply of something available to you regardless of your circumstances, explains Chrissy Papetti, a self-mastery mentor, success coach, and speaker. With this mindset, you truly believe and trust that infinite opportunities, time, resources, money, and love are available to you and that others' gain does not equal your loss. Even if you're having difficulty believing in yourself right now, practice can help you establish a growth mindset. Utilize these abundance mindset exercises to cultivate your strengths and positively impact others.

- **Recognize and accept your flaws.**

  Recognizing your flaws in a healthy, caring manner enables you to develop and learn. After that, you can embark on a path of self-development. Accepting your flaws may forgive yourself and learn from your mistakes rather than berating yourself, blaming others, or spiraling into negative thoughts and actions.

- **Develop your strengths.**

  Everybody has flaws. However, we do have our strengths. When you recognize your personal qualities, you can cultivate them and allow them to shine. This thinking promotes abundance because it acknowledges that everyone has something to offer.

- **Consider your options.**

    To put this into practice, set aside some time each week to imagine what you want to accomplish or your ideal self. Close your eyes and see the scenario unfolding in your favor.
    Consider the following:

- What is conceivable?
- How can the most beautiful and successful solution appear?
- How would success manifest itself? Through imagination, you can visualize yourself living in abundance. Consider balancing your bank account, obtaining that promotion, or cohabiting with your family in a cheerful home.

- **Recognize your internal dialogue.**

    Negative mental patterns, such as emotions of scarcity, typically arise in childhood. They develop into habits and are second nature. Perhaps you were taught that success, financial security, and love were all possible for others but not for you. Take note of your internal discourse. Keep an eye out for negative self-talk. It may be beneficial to document thought patterns for a week or two. Make a note of each time you find yourself in a scarcity mindset. You may notice that particular situations or people elicit those responses.

- **Give**

    If you have a scarcity mindset, you tend to view another person's gain as your loss. Alternatively, an abundant mentality recognizes the unlimited resources available to everyone. You can build an abundant mindset by finding opportunities to give back to others. Giving money or your time teaches you to help others instead of keeping things for yourself.

- ## Optimistic Idea

Positive thinking can be an excellent way to enhance one's confidence. Assume you believe you are capable of accomplishing something.

Then, you are more inclined to work diligently to ensure success. If you doubt your ability to complete a task, you are more likely to approach it half-heartedly and thus be more likely to fail. The trick is convincing oneself to act - with the optimal level of aid, support, preparation, and skill. An optimistic view fosters confidence, which results in accomplishment. Nothing can be accomplished without hope, as well as self-confidence. A wealth of information is available on practical thinking, both online and in print. The appropriate hopefulness policies emphasize your fortitude and accomplishments while compensating for your weaknesses and errors. This is much simpler than it appears, and we frequently dramatize unsatisfactory aspects of our past, making them far more significant problems than they are. These negative ideas can have a detrimental effect on your confidence and capacity to achieve goals.

▪ Shifting perspective

Shifting your perspective can help you deal with situations you don't like or difficulties you can't seem to solve. Shifting your viewpoint can help you focus on the positive, improve your attitude, and generate new ideas. To transform yourself, your situation, or others, you shift perspective by thinking or doing something differently. Teaching yourself to think more positively can assist you in dealing with life's obstacles. **Shifting your perspective isn't easy, but these pointers can help you get started.**

- **Distance Yourself from Negativity** Have you ever noticed how frequently focusing on the negative is more manageable than focusing on the positive? When you're experiencing strong emotions, logic frequently takes a back seat. If the people with whom you spend most of your time are generally negative, it will be nearly impossible to avoid being drawn into their negativity. When it comes to managing the negativity you allow into your life, it is not just about the people in your life. Consider the type of content you consume and the messaging you allow to program your mind subconsciously.

- **Reframe your thoughts.**

Reframing your mental attitude toward everyday occurrences is an easy method to find an optimistic viewpoint in any area of your life. You can discover a silver lining by reminding yourself that you "get to" accomplish something instead of telling yourself that you "have to." "I have to clean the house" has a negative connotation since it portrays cleaning as an unwelcome job. "I get to clean the house," on the other hand, reframes the work as something you're looking forward to, emphasizing the importance of having a place to live in the first place. Reframing chores in your everyday life with a positive mindset is a terrific way to shift your perspective and improve your mental health.

- **Manage Your Expectations**

Unfulfilled expectations result in dissatisfaction. It's infuriating when we expect someone to do something and fail to deliver. We have no control over what others do. However, we can exercise greater control over our expectations. If you expect someone who has demonstrated an inability to follow through on something, you have not set them up for success. To avoid drama in your life due to unmet expectations, ensure that expectations are communicated clearly and that no assumptions are formed.

- **Acknowledge When Something isn't Permanent**

Numerous aspects of life are beyond our control. However, many of the daily dramas we face are transient. You are no longer trapped in the unbearable traffic you were in previously. You can spend less time with a family member who constantly finds new ways to express complicated feelings. The team member who is a source of contention in your organization should be permitted to seek happiness elsewhere. While you cannot change another person's behavior or attitude, you can shift your perspective to see that the drama lasts only as long as you allow it to.

- **Visualize.**

Experiment with seeing the problem from several angles. It enables you to make mental room for a new world. You can begin to see new things if you look at life's challenges in this way, envisioning yourself up close and far away from the difficulty. You have a new perspective on the details. It's possible that things aren't as they appear right now. Alternatively, you might discover the information you require for your next step. You start to notice new details, new roads, and fresh viewpoints.

Because happiness is a state of mind, changing your attitude can significantly impact your happiness.

▪ <u>Be Assertive</u>

Assertiveness entails sticking up for what you believe in and adhering to your convictions. Being assertive implies that you can change your mind if you believe it is correct, not because of external pressure.

Assertiveness and self-confidence are inextricably linked - typically, individuals become much more forceful as their self-confidence grows.

- ## Keep one's cool

Generally, there is a correlation between selfconfidence and tranquillity. If you are enthusiastic about your profession, you will likely be at ease while performing it. If you lack confidence, you are more prone to experience tension or anxiety.
Even when faced with fear and pressure, maintaining a calm mind will make you feel more secure. To achieve this, it is crucial to determine precisely how to relax. Develop at least one beneficial leisure strategy you can utilize when you're stressed; this could be as simple as taking several controlled deep breaths both in and out.

- ## Prevent Arrogance

Conceit is divisive in interpersonal relationships. As your confidence grows and you gain usefulness, resist the need to feel or behave superior to others. Remember that nobody is perfect, and there is always more to learn. Recognize your toughness and also accomplishments, as well as your flaws and also faults. Provide additional credit ratings for their work - be sincere in your comments and admiration. Be kind and respectful, demonstrate an interest in what others are doing, ask questions, seek inclusion, and solicit input from others.

Sustaining Your Confidence

When confronted with a novel situation, the majority of us doubt ourselves. I'm referring to the necessities here; seeing new locales, meeting new people, and even getting a new hairstyle may come under this category. While none of these jobs are complicated, they still cast a pall of self-doubt over us simply because we have not performed them. Most of us can set aside that minor discomfort and progress, but the reality is that we constantly doubt how others perceive us in novel situations, even those we feel relatively insignificant. Now combine those microsecond hunches with a significant unknown, such as discovering new work at a new firm. These great unknowns make us vulnerable, and our confidence level dictates our reactions. Building genuine assurance requires serious effort, which is more difficult because you change your behavior. Thus, your test will ensure that the improvements you make stick.

These are things to know to sustain your confidence:

Quit assuming

Much self-doubt stems from the oblivious convictions and stories we tell ourselves. 'I am sufficiently awful,' and 'I will always be incapable.' Consider this: Are you willing to believe that you must have all of the proper responses before testing a thought? Accept that you will be judged negatively if you raise concerns about aspects of the media plan that aren't working.

Bear in mind that no realities surround this stream; it is purely mental. When you accept this, you will begin to notice advancements.

Acknowledge vacillations

By and large, our confidence fluctuates according to varied conditions, settings, and requirements. Additionally, it might fluctuate based on our perceptions and capacity; this is pretty usual. Confidence is rarely expressed at a high level, regardless of how actively we work to foster it.

Attempt to avoid combating the inescapable!

Reflect routinely

You must regularly assess your confidence levels to determine whether a lack of confidence is holding you back or whether certainty support enables you to step up and into something challenging. Developing experience in assessing your confidence level and influencing your capacity to lead well is critical for sustaining confidence over time. Therefore, make ordinary reflection a habit.

Accept failure

Because we fall off the eating regimen wagon over vacation does not mean we are doomed to return to helpless food patterns for the rest of our lives. Similarly, just because our certainty decreases at some moment does not mean we have completely lost it. This is frequently unavoidable when we allow ourselves to view backsliding as a disappointment. Rather than that, we must remind ourselves that disappointment is an opportunity to grow.

Continue onward

Never let a few days or weeks of reverting to old habits and practices discourage you from reestablishing the behavior you need to modify. Rather than that, return to the cart and utilize what you've learned about how to aid your change. Selfcriticism is a futile exercise that squanders vitality and time, so avoid it!

Act naturally

Appearing genuinely confident for an extended period should be approached from the back. 'Faking it till you make it only takes you to this stage and for an extended time. Attempting to visualize yourself with the confidence necessary to conduct business can be draining. Therefore, figure out how to be you since everyone else is taken, as you are probably aware.

Face being rejected

In media, advertising, and marketing, you must speak up when no one else will and take the initiative to modify. You must be conspicuous and make poor choices. You must be able to stand alone in a crowd, as management is! Indeed, when we rise, we expose ourselves to the risk of denial. Developing your capacity to deal with this is critical, as not everyone will agree with what you have to say.

Reframe problem

Instead of reframing the issue as a healthy debate, most of us see it as inferior. As a result, we keep our ideas to ourselves, hoping we will eventually advance if we keep doing our jobs and delivering the goods. 'Our lives begin to end the day we become silent on vital problems,' said Martin Luther King Jr. So make use of your voice!

Challenge on your own

It would be beneficial if you consistently made points differently tomorrow than you do today. If you've spent the entire day with your head down and bum up,' ripping off your order of business, how are you going to be able to assess what you need to do to succeed? Continue to push yourself and ask, 'If what got me here will not get me there, what do I require to do now to step up and succeed?'

Believe it's worth it.

To achieve a long-lasting change, you must recognize that the benefits of the new behavior outweigh the consequences of continuing to practice the old ones. You must believe that change is worthwhile—because it is.

HAPPINESS

Happiness is a state of mind. It's just according to the way you look at things. – **Walt Disney.**

Everyone in this world is attempting to find happiness in their unique way. Individuals have vastly different character traits, beliefs, religions, values, and ideals, but regardless of which path we take in life, we all want to end up somewhere where we can be happy. Because words are merely symbols, when I use the term "happy," I refer to an enduring joy that permeates your being daily. Happiness, in my usage, refers to a sense of inner peace, joy, bliss, and fulfillment. Happiness is a frame of consciousness defined by the positive and pleasurable influences and emotions encountered during one's lifetime. Happiness is not a singular emotion as contentment or joy are. It is more of a continuum that spans these two emotions.
Simply put, a person who is content with their life is not necessarily happy. Neither does a joyful person, a model of guaranteed happiness. However, a happy person experiences both of these extremes of emotion. Happiness is a choice. A person who

chooses to see the positive side of life and maintains a positive outlook is what we refer to as truly happy. Money, it is said, cannot buy happiness. However, as a friend once said, "Money cannot buy happiness, but it also does not make me sad!"

When I refer to the "secret of happiness," I mean reaching a point in your life where happiness is your default state and is present in your being for the vast majority of the time. To discover the secret of happiness, we must first ask and answer a critical question. What precisely makes a person happy? Individuals have numerous ideas about what they desire in their lives to be happy. For some, financial abundance is the goal; for others, loving relationships are the goal; for others, a sense of fulfillment comes from helping others; for others, success in their chosen career is the goal; and for still others, freedom from oppression or persecution is the goal. A more balanced individual will determine that happiness comes from achieving a certain level of success and harmony in all his significant areas of life, which is far easier said than done. While pursuing these goals may result in varying degrees of external happiness, are they the key to happiness? Let us probe further.

Filling the void will not make you happy.

I'd be content if I could land that new high-paying job. I'd be content if I could escape my small hometown. If I could only find the ideal lover, I would be content. Many people have a single ideal goal that they believe will bring them the happiness they've been seeking. They perceive a certain void in their lives and remain unhappy until that void is filled. The sense of deficiency they carry in this area also contributes to their inability to fulfill it.

Even if you achieve the one thing you believe will make you happy for the rest of your life, it will not dramatically change your circumstances. Sure, you'll experience temporary joy and pride at finally accomplishing what you set out to do. Still, just as quickly as a fancy new car loses its once-exciting appeal, the happiness you gained from accomplishing the goal will fade or be replaced by new goals and desires that you'll be certain will finally make you happy once they're accomplished. One of the reasons you can't find lasting happiness when you accomplish something is your remarkable ability to adapt to your life circumstances. When something is lacking in our lives, we believe that filling the void will provide us with the additional 'thing' we require. However, once the void is filled, we adapt to our new situation, and the other thing becomes the new normal. Our problems or sources of unhappiness are always contextual. A homeless person who receives a sandwich from a stranger may experience the same or greater joy than a businessman who is treated to a fivecourse lobster dinner. Because happiness is relative, it isn't easy to achieve lasting happiness by adding objects, people, or accomplishments to one's life.

What if the preceding does not apply to you? Perhaps you have developed a practice of expressing gratitude for the things in your life and have discovered a way to remain grateful for everything you have without becoming so 'accustomed to them that they lose their appeal. Another underlying issue that jeopardizes your long-term happiness is the impermanence of life.

The impermanence of life

The world is in continuous evolution, and nothing is permanent or eternal. If your happiness is contingent upon your possessions, there is always the fear of losing them. If your happiness is contingent upon your physical appearance, you will eventually grow old and wrinkled. If your happiness is dependent on your friends, family, or lover, they will either die, or we will be separated from them. There is always a way to lose or have taken away what makes you happy. The more we deny this and the harder we fight to keep the things we need, the more unhappy we will be when they are gone. This fact may appear depressing and grim, but this is only true if you believe that happiness must come from all of these external impermanent things. There is only one permanent thing, and it is the trustworthy source of lasting happiness. It may require some effort to locate, but it is free and always available.

<u>Happiness comes from within</u>

Can you be delighted simply by taking a walk in nature? Can you sense tranquillity while sitting alone in silence? Could you still feel pleased if you were stranded on a barren island? Everyone has a default emotional state. What do you feel when there are no external distractions, and your mind is clear of past or future thoughts? Is tranquility your default condition, or is it more damaging, such as boredom, melancholy, or mild annoyance? I know that each of us possesses a profound sense of calm and joy, but often in life, we grow so distant from ourselves that we lose sight of it, and the inner serenity practically vanishes. We become so engrossed with external concerns that we lose sight of the internal. For many people, their minds never allow them to rest. Our heads' near-constant chatter hinders us from perceiving anything inwardly. The secret to permanent happiness is learning to quiet our minds, go within, feel this profound joy, and then bring it out in our daily lives. The constant joy is the only happiness that cannot be stolen or lost. Individuals who have developed the ability to feel good for no reason tap into this source, which is why they are happy while others with better life circumstances may not be. Your happiness is defined by who you indeed are, by yourself. It bears no resemblance to your material belongings, relationships, accomplishments, or even to your physical body. Your pleasure is a natural state of being that exists in the inner recesses of your consciousness. You can ignore it and embrace the world's definition of happiness, but the things you cling to can quickly disappoint, disintegrate, fade, or even vanish from your life. Consider the following. Consider your inner state of happiness as a cake, with tangible goods, accomplishments, and connections serving as the frosting. While the icing adds significantly more to the cake, the cake itself is the actual substance.

How to cultivate inner happiness

A critical step toward cultivating inner peace is to align the voice in your head with the happiness you desire. If your inner thoughts about the outer world are regularly negative, the negativity you generate will isolate you from your inner happiness. Develop the ability to manage your mind and interrupt your thoughts when you discover yourself overthinking negatively. Your mind is only a tool for your use, and it is critical to learn to control it so that it does not dominate you. Develop an optimistic mindset. It requires practice like anything; you must repeat something often before it becomes a habit, but breaking it will undoubtedly improve your life if you have a negative thought pattern. Practice seeing the best in people, the brighter side of things, and being grateful for everything; eventually, thinking positively will be all that remains. The ability to think positively about yourself is critical. Suppose the voice in your head is putting you down, telling you that you're not good enough, that you're incapable of accomplishing something, or simply that you're not a good person. In that case, you'll generate negativity within that suffocates your core positivity. The most critical step toward inner pleasure is learning to love yourself for who you are. Develop into the type of person you'd want to hang out with. As long as you are comfortable spending time alone, it will be easy to feel fantastic for no reason.

Why is happiness a choice?

Happiness appears to be a concept that does not apply to you. How can you choose happiness if you have been harmed and are afflicted by circumstances beyond your control? Each day, we have the option of happiness or misery. The difficulty is that we become trapped by our circumstances. We're having a difficult day at work. We've been in an accident, faced unexpected costs, and encountered other terrible situations. We do not take the big picture into account. We should be pleased with a place to live, transportation, the ability to pay our expenses, and good health. Rather than that, our emotions fluctuate as a result of shifting circumstances. Many people prefer to blame their sadness on their circumstances. Yet, if happiness were just contingent on our circumstances, most people would rarely be happy, as no one lives without sorrow. We all encounter obstacles, setbacks, challenges, and disappointments. It is part of our human existence. While many people are educated and aware, many remain dissatisfied with their lives. Academically, they comprehend the paths to happiness, but knowledge without application is only education. We can study all of the factors that contribute to genuine, lasting pleasure, such as gratitude, forgiveness, love, and service, but little will change unless and until we put them into practice regularly. While a significant portion of your natural disposition toward happiness is dictated by your genetic makeup and hence varies between individuals, it is merely an inherited predisposition, not your fate. What you strive for and accomplish in life is and will always be your destiny. The sensation is a deep-seated sense of spiritual fulfillment. On the other hand, happiness results from a series of choices (consciously or unconsciously). There are several reasons why happiness enhances the enjoyment of life. Your level of happiness, or lack thereof, affects your daily encounters and interpersonal connections. If you're happy, you're much more likely to positively impact your spouse, children, neighbors, friends, workplace, and community. When each of us is at our happiest, the world is a better place.

Happiness is a choice. Each minute spent in anger or frustration results in a loss of 60 seconds of happiness. Sustain a state of contentment. Keep your integrity. Allow individuals to be themselves if they disagree. It is not essential to please everyone in life. You already possess everything necessary for happiness.

CONCLUSION

Numerous individuals have a constant and automatic background of opposing ideas and self-limiting beliefs. Their negative ideas significantly contribute to the unfavorable outcomes in their lives.

Our ideas determine our actions, but we can also control them! By rejecting negative influences, scarcity mindsets, limiting beliefs, and focusing on positive action, we can build a new world for ourselves. This is why you frequently read about success stories that began with adversity and culminated in astounding and life-altering outcomes. These people are similar to you and me. They grabbed the bull by the horns, wrestled it to the ground, climbed to the top, and never descended. Both mental and physical exertion created the expected and desirable outcomes. But they never gave up or allowed criticism to deter them. And this is the crucial point. You will conquer every ounce of dread if you persevere, take action, and enjoy triumphs.

Everyone engages in some form of internal dialogue or self-talk. It frequently provides a running commentary on what we are doing, commenting on our appearance when we gaze in the mirror, observing our behaviors, and providing feedback on our decisions. The problem is that this self-talk is frequently negative, critical, and unproductive, and we do not correct it.

You will discover if you are sensitive to negative thinking patterns or repeating trauma if you begin to pay attention to your thoughts and internal dialogue. If they persist in sabotaging you, begin correcting or eliminating them as they appear. If you can learn to put your mind to work for you, it will assist you in achieving your life goals. Working independently will need practice, but the effort is worth it.

Always remember that:

- Your thoughts become your words.

- Be watchful of your words as they transform into actions.

- Observe your conduct as it develops into a routine.

- Observe your habits because they shape your personality.

- Your character will determine your fate, so be mindful of it.

www.ingramcontent.com/pod-product-compliance
Lightning Source LLC
Chambersburg PA
CBHW062057270326
41931CB00013B/3119